Career Development and Inclusive Practice

Strategies for Inclusive Practice in Career Counselling

Jules Benton and Chris Targett

Career Development and Inclusive Practice

This first edition published in 2024 by Trotman, an imprint of Trotman Indigo Publishing Ltd, 18e Charles Street, Bath, BA1 1HX

© Trotman Indigo Publishing Ltd 2024

Authors: Jules Benton and Chris Targett

British Library Cataloguing in Publication Data
A catalogue record for this book is available from the British Library.

Paperback ISBN 978 1 911724 28 5
Hardback ISBN 978 1 911724 35 3

All rights reserved. This book is sold subject to the condition that it shall not, by way of trade or otherwise, be lent, resold, hired out or otherwise circulated without the publisher's prior written consent in any form of binding or cover other than that in which it is published and without a similar condition including this condition being imposed on the subsequent purchaser. No part of this publication may be reproduced, stored in a retrieval system or transmitted in any form or by any means, electronic and mechanical, photocopying, recording or otherwise without prior permission of Trotman Indigo Publishing.

Every effort has been made to trace copyright holders and to obtain their permission for the use of copyright material. The publisher apologises for any errors or omissions, and would be grateful to be notified of any corrections that should be incorporated in future editions of this book.

Printed and bound in the UK by CMP Ltd

 All details in this book were correct at the time of going to press. To keep up-to-date with all the latest news and updates and to access the online resources that accompany this book, use the QR code or visit **trotman.co.uk/pages/career-development-and-inclusive-practice-resources**

Contents

About the authors	vii
Foreword	ix
Chapter 1 A bit about our book	**1**
Why we wrote it	1
What is in it?	1
What do we mean by Careers Guidance?	2
Format	3
Disability and learning support needs	4
About us	4
Taking a very personal view	5
Chapter 2 Regulate, relate and communicate	**7**
Ideas for a sensory toolkit	9
Sight	11
Hearing	13
Assisted communication	21
Asking questions	23
Chapter 3 'Disability'	**31**
Models of Disability	32
How does disability affect decision-making?	35
Chapter 4 Impairment and adjustments	**37**
Making reasonable adjustments to Career Guidance	37
Making changes to the environment	38
Making changes to the format of support	39
Changes to how we provide information	41
Action plans	41
Speech	43
Sign language	47
Chapter 5 Navigate the systems of support	**49**
Support in learning	49
Wales	50
England	51
Northern Ireland	52
Supported internships	53
Inclusive apprenticeships	53

Higher education	54
Support for job seekers	56
What other support is available?	57
Grants, bursaries and charitable organisations	58
Transition from children's to adults' services	58

Chapter 6 Ethics and agendas — 61

Impartiality and transparency	61
Reflective practice	62
Why is reflective practice good for us and our clients?	63
Dialogue	63
Inclusivity within ethics	66
Common challenges	69
Government agendas	77
Education agendas	78
Funding	79
Media	80

Chapter 7 Creating individualised approaches — 83

Self	83
Opportunities	87
Decisions	90
Transitions	92
'Important to'	92
Supporting families	93
Just one thing	94

Chapter 8 How we organise interactions — 99

Length of session	99
Introducing . . .	99
Fixed but flexible	101
Drop-Ins	101
Flexed appointments	103
Thirty-minute fixed session (with repeats)	103
Room set-up	105
Someone else in the room?	107
Circles of support	108

Chapter 9 Action planning and information sharing — 117

Action planning	117
SMART/Er	118
Diversify the questions	120

Thinking differently	121
Triggers and blockers	121
Punk action planning	122
Do it together	124
Time	124
Back-up plans	124
Sharing action plans	125
Information sharing	126
Enthusiastic consent!	126
Inclusive approaches to action planning	129
Inclusive by design	129
Colours matter	130
Person-centred planning	131
PATH, MAPS and circles	132
Cloud map	134

Chapter 10 Using theory in our practice — **137**

Sensory integration theory	142
Play theory	142
Our 'Relate' Model	143

Chapter 11 Legislate and advocate — **149**

Policy and legislation	149
Equality and discrimination	149
Mental capacity	150
Mental capacity and learning support	152
Safeguarding	153
Human rights	154
Advocacy	155
Learning support, transition and preparing for adulthood	155
Telling others about an impairment or health condition	157

Glossary	**159**
Resources and further information	**179**
Afterword and acknowledgements	**207**

About the authors

Chris Targett
Chris Targett is a dynamic and innovative careers adviser who received the CDI's 'UK Careers Adviser of the Year' Award in 2021. His background in art and philosophy informs his creative approach, supporting young people, schools and colleagues across the guidance community. Chris currently works as an area manager & careers adviser for the charity CXK, and he is also Chair of the Careers Writers Association (CWA).

Jules Benton
Jules Benton has over 35 years' experience working as a careers guidance professional, trainer and consultant. She specialises in delivering training on careers guidance for individuals who are disabled, have learning support needs or experience other barriers to inclusion. Jules is also Chief Executive of Cosmic Cactus, a service that provides support for transitions to employment, training and education.

Foreword

All clients have individual needs, and some clients also have additional needs. Knowing how to meet these needs in ways that are safe and comfortable for all our clients is a vital aspect of inclusive practice.

Reading this book will not only enable you to understand the range of strategies and techniques that can be used to engage with clients with learning and additional needs but also show you how these can be used with neurotypical and non-disabled individuals.

For anyone working in the career development sector or allied areas, this book will enhance your understanding of different conditions and how these affect each individual in different ways, improve your ability to communicate effectively with all of your clients and enable them to feel at ease and happy to work with you.

Drawing on the vast experience of its authors, this book buzzes with such enthusiasm about all its content that it can easily be read from cover to cover as well as being one that can be returned to time and again as a reference source. It is also an excellent tool to use to truly reflect on how you work with clients and to ask yourself how inclusive your practice actually is.

If you are new to working in the career development sector, studying a career development qualification or have worked in the sector for many years, this book will increase your confidence and enhance your understanding of how to engage effectively and ethically with all the multifaceted individuals who make our working lives such a privilege.

It is also a valuable source of information for those who fund and manage provision, as it shows how employing professionally qualified staff and giving them the time and resources needed for the role can lead to all clients being enabled to pursue a career path that is right for them.

I am delighted that this book is now available, as it draws together so many sources of information and inspiration into one very accessible document, and I have no hesitation in recommending this motivating book to everyone.

Claire Johnson, RCDP and CDI, ICCI and NICEC Fellow.
CDI Head of Professional Development and Standards.
November 2024

Chapter 1
A bit about our book

Why we wrote it

Initial training for Career Guidance Professionals has limited content on how to make adjustments to our practice to be inclusive of people with an impairment, health condition, learning support need or disabling factor.

This is a source of anxiety for many.

We can feel:

- we won't know enough about the person's impairment and how this affects career planning;
- we don't have the tools or strategies to adapt our guidance processes;
- inadequate in our communication skills;
- high expectations of others involved in the person's life planning; and
- inexperienced in the systems that impact the person – assessment, plans, health services, benefits, funding, support options.

This book aims to explore how career guidance can be successfully adapted to meet a variety of needs from the perspective of practitioners.

What is in it?

The book includes:

- our perception of 'disability' or 'learning support' and how this affects the delivery of effective career guidance;
- other people's perception of us, how a person's impairment might affect this and how this can impact the delivery of effective career guidance;
- effective communication – including techniques and adjustments that can help when working with clients who have selective mutism, sensory processing needs or learning difficulties;
- decision-making processes . . . what gets in the way? How do we make decisions? Does disability affect planning and decision-making? How can we support decision-making in others?

- how reflective practice, and a good working knowledge of underpinning theories, helps us to be more inclusive;
- strategies that have worked to overcome specific challenges such as non-verbal communication and literacy difficulties;
- working with a circle of support for individuals who choose not to, or are unable to, make independent decisions;
- person-centred planning, mental capacity, advocacy and preparing for adulthood;
- the range and efficacy of resources and tools we use;
- case studies to illustrate approaches and impact (anonymised with fictitious names);
- signposting to other resources that can support the careers practitioner and their clients in the career planning process;
- some reflections on our values and ethics; and
- a resources section that can be accessed online.

What do we mean by Careers Guidance?

In this book, when we refer to Careers Guidance (called 1:1 Personal Guidance in the Gatsby Benchmarks).

This is Careers Guidance provided by a qualified career development professional, who subscribes to the CDI – or equivalent professional body – Code of Ethics.

> Careers practitioners call themselves many different things, from careers advisers through to career development professionals, careers counsellors or careers coaches. We have settled on using the term 'careers practitioner' to encompass all these definitions, as a broad label, and career development professional to describe someone fully qualified to deliver guidance.

The approaches we offer are not exclusive to careers practitioners. We hope those in related sectors and professions find our suggestions useful to consider in their work. Teachers, Learning Support staff, Employability Coaches, Career Leaders, Youth Workers, Social Workers, Counsellors and Psychotherapists are all welcome! We are keen to produce a guide that will support others in working with a range of clients.

Many of the approaches we present build upon the training that leads to the status of careers practitioners being registered career development professionals (RCDP) within the Career Development Institute, our professional body. Therefore, we won't include in-depth discussions of the relevant foundational models and theories based on existing training, unless doing so expands upon the points we are making.

We have included some brief summaries and a reading list in the resources section, where you can rediscover some of the models and theories we refer to.

Format

The book is a mixture of discussions concerning the challenges practitioners face when working with clients who have a variety of support needs, as well as practical examples of possible solutions and tools, you may wish to implement or try in your own career practice.

Our intention is for you to find strategies congruent to you and your authentic self. What we know, from helping to guide and develop practitioners, is that when you attempt to practice like someone else, or try to be someone else, the strength of your practice diminishes.

> While reading this book, please feel free to disagree with us, pick and choose what resonates with you in your work, and question us.
>
> Both of us are happy to discuss ideas and issues raised within the book – contact us via whichever communication method suits you.

We will mix theory, personal reflections, anecdotes, research and case studies to help illustrate ideas and suggestions. Our hope is that practitioners will be able to dive in and out of the sections of the book as they need to.

The resources section has links to lots of further information and tools to add to your toolkit. You can access it via the QR code and URL at the start of the book.

For some explanations about different impairments, and some of the words and phrases used within learning support and disability communities, have a look at our glossary.

Whether you are an experienced practitioner or newly qualified, this book will broaden your practice and be a companion on your journey.

Reflective practice is used as a tool to examine why techniques may or may not work.

We ask you to:

- listen in order to understand others, rather than to plan what you're going to say;
- suspend judgement and criticism;
- respect the views of others and their right to hold them;
- share your own ideas with colleagues and clients;
- challenge yourself constructively; and
- be prepared to experiment.

Disability and learning support needs

Our intention is not to segregate techniques and approaches for those with 'additional needs' and those without. However, we will look at the dividing lines that society creates related to learning support needs and disability, being mindful that these can influence our practice and put up barriers where there need not be any.

We will focus on client-centred practice and approaches, considering how impairments or conditions may manifest for an individual.

What is crucial is that we ask our clients how their needs manifest for them, how they impact them in different environments and whether they agree the support and types of approaches work best for them.

Although this book focuses on disability, we hope it promotes inclusion in its widest sense.

About us

Jules is currently Chief Executive of Cosmic Cactus – a company formed in November 2021 to provide Information, Advice, Guidance and Person-centred Support for Transition to Employment, Training, FE/HE and Adult Services. Cosmic Cactus works mainly, but not exclusively, in the Dorset Council area.

The focus of Cosmic Cactus is people who experience barriers to participation (such as discrimination, prejudice, disability, impairment, health issues, special educational needs, exclusion, marginalisation etc.)

Jules has over 35 years' experience working within the Public, Private and Voluntary, Community and Social Enterprise sectors as a manager of people and projects, Career Guidance Professional, trainer and consultant. She is the parent of two young adults, both of whom are neurodivergent.

Jules regularly delivers training on Careers Education, Information, Advice and Guidance for people with an impairment, health condition or learning support need, for organisations such as the Career Development Institute, Disability Rights UK and regional careers hubs, networks and companies. Jules is currently delivering the Career Development Institute training for qualified career development professionals who work with students who have learning support needs and/or are disabled.

Chris has worked in education since 2001 in various roles, including as a student mentor and personal tutor. He has worked as a career development professional since 2006, amassing a wealth of knowledge and experience, for which he has been recognised nationally (winning the CDI UK Careers Adviser of the Year 2021).

As a manager and career development professional for leading South-East charity CXK, he works across a wide variety of contexts, including mainstream and specialist schools and colleges, ranging from independent through to non-selective, academy and grammar based, as well as specialist settings for students with learning support needs. In addition, he is involved in the training and development of careers practitioners via professional development workshops and speaks regularly at conferences for careers practitioners locally and nationally.

He has helped to develop resources for use by clients and practitioners which are inclusive by design, as well as other media content for the CXK Careers Hub (a careers resource portal), which includes the CXK YouTube channel.

Local projects and initiatives he has been involved with include input into the Kent County Council Local Offer, as well as, support and involvement in the Kent & Medway Progression Federation (KMPF) Special Educational Needs and Disability Progression Partnership projects. This involvement includes contributing to the development of resources for those with additional needs and their families, carers and/or guardians.

He has 'ADHD' (via a late diagnosis as an adult) and two children who have ADHD/C and ASC, both of whom have had very different experiences with the education system.

Taking a very personal view

It is worth noting, in this book you won't see 'Chapters by Chris' and 'Chapters by Jules' as it is a blend of both our voices and experiences, creating a shared voice. However, you may find that where one of us has more experience or expertise, their voice may lead within those areas.

This book does not necessarily represent the views of our employers, or the professional bodies we are part of, and is intended as a guide for practice and reflection rather than a rule book of approaches set in stone.

We are aware that as new approaches develop and understanding within this area expands, some ideas may age and become outdated. Our long-term hope is that this book will become redundant, as the practical, creative and client-centred approaches we discuss become widely known, used and developed further in careers practice.

We have written with unconditional positive regard for you as our reader and without judgement.

We hope you find it a useful guide wherever you practice, helping you to increase your confidence as you grow in your daily career practice and client work.

With best wishes, Jules and Chris
Autumn 2024

Chapter 2
Regulate, relate and communicate

The ability to communicate requires complex skills, and many different parts of the brain are involved.

> **A bit about brains**

The cerebral cortex (the outer part of the brain) is responsible for our more sophisticated thinking skills.

The frontal lobes – 'executive functions', including planning, organisation, flexible thinking and social behaviour.

Other parts of the brain interact to perform skills.

Any condition affecting your brain can cause difficulties with:

- attention and concentration;
- memory;
- literal interpretation, for example, differences/damage on the right side of the brain may lead to the person interpreting verbal information very concretely and taking things literally. They may struggle to understand humour or sarcasm and may miss the nuances of conversation.
- reduced reasoning and problem-solving skills; and
- information processing.

Try to notice when clients:

- are overly talkative or 'hog' the conversation;
- don't realise that it is their turn to speak;

- interrupt because they are afraid they will 'forget what they want to say';
- flit from topic to topic;
- speak only about themselves or fixate on certain subjects;
- talk in a sexually explicit way or swear at inappropriate times;
- perseverate (become stuck) on a topic;
- assume that you share knowledge about a topic; and
- don't 'read' non-verbal cues;
    - ✔ These can all be indicators of brain differences or injury, and you may need to adapt your own communication.

We have placed some links in the resources section if you would like to learn more about brain differences and brain injury.

> An effective communication is where the intended message is successfully **delivered, received and understood.**

Career Guidance is a process founded on effective communication. In order to communicate effectively, people – that includes both careers practitioners and our clients – need first to be regulated.

When dysregulated, we can't focus on communication activities.

Our bodies (and brains) regulate in response to sensory information.

If over-alert, we can become overwhelmed and 'freeze' or go into 'fight' or 'flight' mode.

If under-alert, our brains can go on 'standby' or fall asleep.

As career practitioners we want our clients to be calm, alert, to feel safe in their environment and maintain attention.

The way we are taught to interview usually begins with engaging/relating to a person (often involving chat or small talk – 'hello, how are you today?', 'nice weather' etc.)

We then move into contracting, exploring, questioning – the 'reasoning' part.

However, if we try to move into these before someone is regulated, we risk non-engagement.

- Remember to . . . **Regulate** → **Relate** → **Reason**
- To offer people the opportunity to regulate . . . offer options to engage with sensory resources.

Ideas for a sensory toolkit

This could include:

- fidget toys for times when staying seated or still, or 'waiting', is necessary. Fidget toys are also excellent for assisting with self-regulation and moments of anxiety and stress.
- proprioceptive tools which offer a bit of physical work, such as clay, play dough, a stress ball or balloon filled with sand and knotted securely;
- tools to provide deep pressure touch, such as a weighted blanket, cushion or toy;
- visually soothing toys and gadgets . . . such as a liquid motion bubbler or spinning toy;
- visual or tactile prompts for activity – cards and games:
    - ✔ These can be careers related, for example, *What's Your Strength?*, *Career Navigator*, *Shape of Careers*, *I Don't Know!*, *Panjango*

- visual timetables;
- a portable timer to help with transitions;
- fine motor and visual motor-based activities, such as pencils, scented markers, pegboard, Etch a Sketch, Lego, puzzles, Minecraft, Roblox, chess;
- things to use for 'scaling' or demonstrating concepts visually, such as an old set of keys, pipe cleaners, stones, buttons, ribbons, beads;
- tools for defensiveness include noise-cancelling headphones, a floppy hat, sunglasses, earplugs and/or nose plugs;
- metaphorical prompts – toys, objects or pictures which can have 'meaning' attached to them;
- move! Offer a walk and talk, swap chairs;
- visit the sensory room or quiet room in your setting and find out how to book it for clients who might need it.

A bit about our senses

Sensory information is any message that we receive from our senses.

This includes the five senses that most of us are familiar with: taste, smell, sight, hearing and touch.

In addition, we receive information from our proprioceptive and vestibular senses.

The cells in our body that sense proprioception are located in our muscles and joints, and they process sensory information when our body moves.

The vestibular system receives information when our head moves. When the vestibular system doesn't process the information it receives very well, people could either respond by seeking out more movement or by just being slow to respond.

For people with sensory processing challenges, such as those with vision or hearing impairments, autism spectrum conditions (ASC), attention deficit hyperactivity disorder (ADHD) or sensory processing disorder (SPD), difficulties in sensory regulation can significantly impact their engagement, communication and their ability to make decisions or plan.

They may (depending on which senses are under- or overstimulated):

- struggle to filter out background sensory stimuli – sounds, movement outside windows;
- fail to notice extreme odours (this can include their own body odour) or dislike people/places with distinctive smells;
- have difficulty getting to sleep – which affects their ability to engage and concentrate;
- self-harm;
- only tolerate certain types of clothing or textures;
- stand too close to others because they cannot measure their proximity to other people and judge personal space;
- seem afraid of escalators, lifts or having their hair washed;
- pursue movement – sometimes to the point it interferes with daily routines;
- rock in their chair or while standing, fiddle or tap;
- seek extreme motion;
- appear 'clumsy'.
    - ✔ Our brain *interprets* what we see, hear, touch, smell and feel. So, we all experience the world differently!

Sight

Our eyes are continuously bombarded with visual information – shapes, colours and motion. We also blink, move our eyes, heads and bodies.

Our brains try to make sense of this for us. Look at any 'optical illusion' to see how we perceive things that simply aren't there and don't see things that are!

In addition to this, many people have specific visual impairments.

There are hundreds of different types of eye conditions.

A few of the most common conditions that you are likely to hear about include:

- age-related macular degeneration;
- cataracts;
- glaucoma;
- diabetic retinopathy;
- retinitis pigmentosa;

- refractive error – this term covers several eye conditions which can usually be corrected by glasses or contact lenses, for example, myopia (short-sightedness) or hypermetropia (long-sightedness).

What do we mean by blind?

Many blind people have light perception, meaning they can distinguish between light and dark. In the UK, ophthalmologists (hospital eye doctors) decide if someone can be registered as severely sight impaired (SSI) or sight impaired (SI). Registration involves consideration of the degree to which a person's central and peripheral vision (also known as side vision) is reduced.

The terms 'severely sight impaired' and 'sight impaired' are medical terms. Most people use the terms 'blind' and 'partially sighted'.

What is colour blindness?

Colour blindness = colour vision deficiency (CVD)

In the UK, there are approximately three million colour-blind people (about 4.5% of the entire population), most of whom are male.

It is mostly genetic, although some people become colour blind as a result of other diseases (such as diabetes and multiple sclerosis), or it can be acquired due to ageing or from taking drugs and medications.

There are several types of colour blindness.

How do visuals help us and our clients?

- Visual schedules and pictures can enhance communication for individuals with autism and other sensory processing difficulties.
- Vision is also important in reading body language and other non-verbal cues during social interactions.
- People with a hearing impairment may rely on lip-reading.
- Many people remember pictures more easily than words.
- Watching and listening (videos, podcasts, etc.) removes the necessity to 'read'.

Things to consider:

- Colour is used extensively in learning and education (including Careers resources). For colour-blind people, this can hinder their learning, solely because they aren't able to distinguish accurately between many colours (not just reds and greens – that's a myth)!
- Insufficient contrast between text and background colour makes reading really difficult for many visually impaired and colour-blind people.

- There are lots of ways to make services and products more accessible. Does your organisation do this? Chapter 4 gives some ideas on how you can make reasonable adjustments.

Hearing

Our ears are important for both hearing and balance.

How do ears work?

Sound waves are collected by the pinna (outer ear) on each side of our head and are funnelled into the ear canals. These sound waves make the eardrum vibrate.

The eardrum's vibrations move tiny bones (the ossicles – malleus, incus and stapes) in the middle ear, transferring the sound vibrations into the cochlea of the inner ear.

The stapes sits in a membrane-covered window in the bony wall that separates the middle ear from the cochlea of the inner ear. As the stapes vibrates, it makes the fluids in the cochlea move in a wave-like manner. This stimulates tiny 'hair cells'.

The 'hair cells' are tuned to respond to different sounds based on their pitch or frequency. High-pitched sounds will stimulate 'hair cells' in the upper part of the cochlea. Low-pitched sounds will stimulate 'hair cells' in the lower part of the cochlea.

When each 'hair cell' detects, it generates nerve impulses. These travel along the auditory nerve.

The nerve impulses go through the brainstem before arriving at the hearing centres of the brain, the auditory cortex. This is where they are converted into meaningful sound.

All of this happens within a fraction of a second!

What's happening when you have problems with your hearing?

Hearing well depends on all parts of our auditory system working normally. This ensures that sound can pass through the different parts of the ear to the brain to be processed without any distortion. The type of hearing problem you have depends on which part of your auditory system is not responding well.

Hearing loss and deafness happen when sound signals don't reach the brain. This is caused by a problem in the hearing system. There are two main types of hearing loss. It's possible to have both types, and this is known as mixed hearing loss.

Sensorineural hearing loss is caused by damage to the hair cells inside the inner ear, damage to the hearing nerve or both. It makes it more difficult to hear quiet sounds and reduces the quality of sound that you can hear. Sensorineural hearing loss is permanent but can often be supported by hearing aids.

Conductive hearing loss happens when a problem with the ear, such as ear wax or an ear infection, stops sound from passing through to the cochlea (the hearing organ). Sounds will become quieter and may sound muffled. It can be temporary or permanent, depending on the cause. Conductive hearing loss is usually caused by ear problems.

Ear problems include:

- earwax build-up;
- ear infections;
- glue ear;
- damaged ossicles – serious ear infections and head injuries can damage the ossicles (tiny bones) in the middle ear that pass sound waves from the eardrum to the inner ear, causing hearing loss.
- otosclerosis – Otosclerosis is caused when abnormal bone growth sticks one of the ossicles (stapes) to other parts of the ear.
- perforated eardrum;
- cholesteatoma – an abnormal collection of skin cells in the space behind the eardrum (the middle ear);
- exostosis (surfer's ear) – bony swellings (exostoses) grow slowly over time, causing the ear canal to become narrower.

What causes hearing loss?

Age-related hearing loss is caused by changes that happen over time to the inner ear and is the most common cause of hearing loss.

Sudden hearing loss can be caused by earwax, ear infections, physical injury, side effects of medication, acoustic neuromas and Ménière's disease.

Loud noises can damage the cochlea (hearing organ), causing permanent hearing loss and tinnitus. Exposure to loud noise is the second biggest cause of hearing loss.

Some types of deafness can be inherited, caused by genetic changes.

Some medicines (called ototoxic medicines) have side effects that can cause damage to the cochlea (hearing organ) or the balance system in the inner ear. This can lead to hearing loss, balance problems or tinnitus.

An acoustic neuroma (also known as a vestibular schwannoma) is a rare, slow-growing tumour that grows on the hearing and balance nerves.

Do our ears deceive us?

The McGurk effect occurs when a person perceives that another's lip movements do not correspond to what that individual is saying. This can lead to the perception that the person is saying something different.

Factors that can influence this effect include visual distraction, tactile diversion, familiarity, syllable structure, brain damage, Alzheimer's disease, Specific Language Impairment and aphasia.

Tinnitus is the name for hearing noises that do not come from an outside source.

It can sound like ringing, buzzing, whooshing, humming, hissing, throbbing, music or singing.

Hallucinations and hearing voices

Hallucinations are when you hear, see, smell, taste or feel things that appear to be real but only exist in your mind.

Hallucinations can be caused by many different things that affect the senses, including:

- mental health conditions (like schizophrenia or bipolar disorder);
- drugs and alcohol;
- Alzheimer's or Parkinson's disease;
- a change or loss of vision (such as Charles Bonnet syndrome);
- anxiety, depression or bereavement;
- side effects of medicines;
- anaesthesia;
- migraines;
- a high temperature;
- infection;
- brain tumour;
- confusion;

or just as you wake up or fall asleep.

What is d/Deaf or hard of hearing?

People who are d/Deaf or hard of hearing may have difficulty learning to speak, and their communication skills could be less developed than people of a similar age and ability. This may also affect their ability to read and write. Severe hearing loss causes a person to speak with an intonation different from hearing people. Profoundly d/Deaf people frequently use sign language instead of speech to communicate. For many, this is their first language and sometimes their only one. Some people use a combination of residual hearing (with aids), lip-reading and sign language. Most d/Deaf people are not expert lip-readers but use it to support their residual hearing.

Support could include a communicator, induction loops for meetings, tablets, specialist teachers and support workers for note-taking.

How can we be more inclusive?

- Face the source of light when speaking; this is especially important to allow a d/Deaf person to lip-read.
- Look at the person when speaking.
- Speak clearly and keep your hands clear of your mouth.
- Speak in short sentences.
- Keep the sentence structure simple.
- Start sentences with a keyword; it can be useful to write this word down.
- Use gestures and facial expressions to enhance the meaning of words.
- Visual aids can be useful: handouts, drawings, photographs of people at work. Do not be afraid to write things down.
- Re-phrase a sentence rather than repeat the same words.
- Do not shout!
- Be aware of 'body language'.
- Use an interpreter where appropriate.
- Good lighting is important.
- Reduce or eliminate background noise.
- Provide d/Deaf awareness training for staff.
- Offer a hearing loop system for individuals with hearing aids.
- Appoint a member of staff who can communicate in BSL or use Makaton to support spoken language.

Deaf with a capital D is most commonly used to refer to a person with a hearing loss so profound that they have barely any or no functional hearing. It is also used to describe people who are active members of the Deaf community and identify themselves as culturally Deaf.

Deaf people see their deafness as an identity, not a disability – the affirmation model of disability is explained in Chapter 3. They value their Deaf identity and take great pride in being who they are. For them, Deaf (with an uppercase 'D') is a sign of a cultural identity for people with hearing loss who share a mutual culture and language with each other.

deaf (with a lowercase 'd')

Anyone who cannot understand speech (with or without hearing aids or other devices) using sound alone is deaf.

The 'lowercase d' deaf is simply the medical and audiological definition for having hearing loss, which may differ in severity from one person to another.

The sociological and cultural definitions of the term are different from the medical and audiological definitions. People who are deaf (with a lowercase 'd') are often those who don't identify themselves with the Deaf community. It is also more likely that they don't use sign language as a means of communication and prefer to rely more on oral communication.

Hard of hearing

Hard of hearing is a widely accepted term to describe someone with mild-to-moderate hearing loss.

People may use hearing aids, an FM system, cochlear implants and/or other assistive listening devices to enhance their hearing. In addition, they may rely on lip-reading and/or subtitles or captioning.

Hearing-impaired

The term 'hearing-impaired' is often used to describe people with **any** degree of hearing loss.

Because there is a negative meaning attached to the term 'impaired', people may prefer 'Deaf', 'deaf' or 'hard of hearing'.

D/Deaf, d/Deafened, d/Deafblind or hard-of-hearing friendly

Employers and/or training providers could offer support, including:

the types of support that will be useful for an individual who is d/Deaf or hard of hearing will vary from person to person. It is important to ask individuals about the ways in which their d/Deafness or disability affects their experience of work and what support they find most useful and effective. Many people who are d/Deaf or hard of hearing will not describe or consider themselves to be disabled. Therefore, it is best practice to refer to people who are d/Deaf and people with disabilities in recruitment materials, training and so on.

Touch
Tactile or touch strategies can have a grounding effect and help the individual understand their body positioning or body in space.

We rarely touch others in our work; however, offering things to touch or hold, such as a cushion or plushie, can have a 'grounding' effect.

Movement and balance
The vestibular system, located in the inner ear, provides information about the position and movement of the head concerning gravity. Physical activities like swinging or bouncing can help individuals regulate their sensory systems.

> A young person who struggled to communicate verbally but was clearly keen to engage used a bouncy castle to regulate. We had their career interview while bouncing. It was challenging (no note-taking) but worked a treat.

As an adviser, you can make environmental modifications:

Creating sensory-friendly environments by adjusting light, noise levels and textures can contribute to improved communication outcomes.

We often become accustomed to familiar settings (office, careers room), and for those of us able to filter out unwanted sensory input or not prone to sensory overload, this becomes something we fail to notice.

- Consider your space as if you were new to it.
- What do you see, hear, smell, feel?
- Ask your clients.
- Adjust accordingly . . . or find another room . . . if there is too much sensory information.

Mindfulness and sensory awareness
Mindfulness practices that heighten sensory awareness can contribute to improved self-regulation and communication skills. This will differ from person to person but learning a few simple techniques to share with clients is useful.

- Do be mindful when being mindful though! Some things which are often used – such as using a bell or chime to indicate the start or end of a meditation – may be dysregulating to an individual with sound sensitivity.

Simple breathing techniques can reduce anxiety before or during an intervention, and once learnt, can be used subsequently when anxiety kicks in (before a job interview or exam, for example).

Breathing techniques help to connect you with your body, calm your nervous system, slow down your heart rate, lower blood pressure and reduce stress in your body.

They can be usefully employed in a range of situations – by us and by our clients:

- to calm yourself down when faced with stress or feeling overwhelmed;
- before you need to respond to a high-stress situation;
- when trying to sleep;
- to reduce work stress;
- to reset your creative juices;
- when you need to clear your head;
- when making plans or setting goals;
- when making a big decision.

One technique is square breathing, also referred to as the box-breathing technique, 4×4 breathing, four-square breathing and four-part breath.

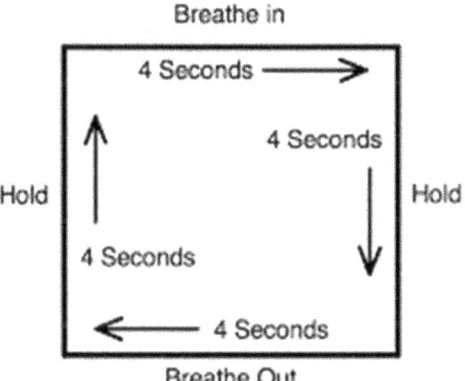

- Sit in a comfortable position.
- Begin by slowly exhaling all of your air out.
- Then, gently inhale through your nose to a slow count of 4.
- Hold at the top of the breath for a count of 4.
- Then gently exhale through your mouth for a count of 4.
- At the bottom of the breath, pause and hold for the count of 4.
- Visualising a square can help – there are lots of images and animations online which can be useful when you practice this technique.

Too much information

Sometimes a person may behave in a way that you wouldn't immediately link to sensory differences. A person who finds it difficult to process everyday sensory information can experience sensory overload or information overload. Too much information can cause stress, anxiety and possibly physical pain. This can result in withdrawal, distressed behaviour or meltdowns.

If you would like to find out what this feels like, try the Autism TMI Virtual Reality Experience.

We often try to impart a lot of information as part of a careers intervention. We think we are being helpful; that if we don't give people all the information, we aren't doing our job properly; and sometimes it is a way of filling silences.

- Find a variety of ways to give information that avoid saying it **at** people and hoping they will process and remember.
- Teach them the skills to find the information they need: ask someone in their circle of support to help them find it; write it; send a link to a video; draw a picture; take a photo; make a voice recording. There is a great video on YouTube that gives some strategies on skills-focused interventions. Go to our resources section to follow the link.
- Do not keep rephrasing – a couple of attempts at clarity is enough to find out if you are making yourself understood.
- Ask if they need more time to think.
- Get comfortable with silence. Some people are naturally 'silence fillers' – if you are one of those, you will need to practice. Counting (silently – in your head) is a useful technique when you first start practising.
- Be aware of the power dynamic – when people perceive you as an 'expert' or person in 'authority', they may be unwilling to ask questions, say they are unclear, or challenge. Be explicit – tell them you welcome questions and that you may not always have made things clear.
- Don't expect people to maintain concentration – some of us are more easily distracted than others.
- Explain the words you use – many words have several meanings or are difficult to understand. There is a nice glossary in the MENCAP guide if you need to explain words related to learning support needs and disability support.
- Avoid jargon and acronyms.
- If you are making a joke . . . say so. Humour is a fantastic tool, but not everyone will understand when you are joking. Sarcasm is not humour.
- Think about how you ask questions.

Speech

Not everyone likes speaking – even if they can.

> *Speech is an odd one for me. Sometimes I lose it and it's very frustrating. Other times it goes away and it's not a problem.*
> *I wish life allowed the second scenario more often. But in reality, I need speech even if I don't always like it.*
>
> ~ Jamie Knight

To find out more, visit Jamie's website, Spaced Out and Smiling, to explore what it means to be 'Autistically happy & sharing what we learn as we transition to independent living'.

People can struggle with the rhythm of a conversation.

> *When several people are together and having a good time, their speech and laughter follow a rhythm . . . I usually interrupt conversations without realising my mistake. The problem is I can't follow the rhythm.*
>
> ~ Temple Grandin

You may need to give parameters to enable people to engage in conversation. This might be:

- an agreed pattern of talking and listening, for example, 'I will ask a question – you answer. Then you ask a question and I will answer'.
- a set amount of time to talk works for some people – egg timers are useful for this;
- an explicit prompt such as 'I'm done talking, your turn'.

Some will be unable to speak at times, so have strategies in place such as rhetorical questions, assistive technology and communication support. [Some common speech and language difficulties are covered at the end of this chapter because this is one of the things we find most challenging within career conversations.]

Assisted communication

AT and AAC

Assistive technology (AT) is any item, piece of equipment, software programme or product system that is used to increase, maintain or improve functional capabilities.

Augmentative and Alternative Communication (AAC) refers to using communicative systems that augment a message and may be alternative to speech.

Effective use of AT and AAC can be empowering:

- If you know you will be working with people who use AT/AAC, request some time in class or with a speech therapist to familiarise yourself with different communication mechanisms.
- Ask if your clients need to bring their AT/AAC aids with them when appointments are booked.
- Allow enough time for interventions.

There is a good selection of free AT available.

- Dark themes can increase concentration time and reduce visual stress. Microsoft Office has dark themes for Word, Outlook, Excel and OneNote.
- If using Word on a tablet, you can also use Voice Control for speech recognition and Read Aloud to have your work read back to you.
- Typing suggestions and word prediction can be used in any application to support learners with a specific learning difficulty to work efficiently.
- Explore screen display and preferred setups for those with sight issues.
- Immersive Reader supports text-to-speech.
- Dictate on the Home tab in Word allows speech recognition.
- Notes (which comes as part of iOS) on an iOS device allow a microphone to be used for speech recognition and convert spoken content from speech to text.
- Google Docs has Voice Typing tools.

Translators, communication support workers (CSW) and interpreters

We might use these words interchangeably, but they are all different.

- A sign language interpreter (or BSL interpreter) is someone who has trained to translate between English and British Sign Language. They **interpret** simultaneously what is being said or spoken into BSL for a deaf person and what is being signed in BSL into spoken English for a hearing person. An interpreter does not translate word for word or sign for sign but uses their knowledge and skills in both languages to translate the content of the signer and speaker into each respective language.
- **Communication Support Workers** (CSWs) are different from interpreters in that they are not professionally trained to

interpret between English and BSL. Their role is to enable access to communication between deaf and hearing people by using a variety of support strategies and communication modes to match the individuals' needs and/or preferences. CSWs are most often used in schools, colleges and universities to help deaf students communicate with their peers and staff. CSWs provide communication support through sign language, note-taking or lip-reading/lip-speaking.

- A **translator** is a person whose job is to change words, especially written words, into a different language.

If you are working with someone who assists a person's communication, check if they have the relevant qualifications, knowledge and skills to support your interventions.

- Whether you are using assistive tech or a person to help with communication, you will need to allow more time to accommodate the extra steps in the communication process.

For more about British Sign Language and other forms of signing, skip to the end of Chapter 4.

Asking questions

Asking too many questions at once and not allowing enough time to answer can overwhelm the other person.

Instead, ask one question at a time and try not to speak over someone when they're replying. For longer or more introspective answers, allow them some extra thinking time, too. And if you need them to elaborate, sometimes a brief pause is all it takes to prompt someone to expand on their answer.

Allow time for processing: Ask your question then . . .

➡ WAIT ➡   REPEAT/REPHRASE if necessary   ➡ WAIT ➡

There are various questioning techniques you can use to gain the information you need. Each technique has its own pros and cons.

- **Closed** questions are useful when you need a to-the-point answer, whereas **open** questions are good for extracting more detailed responses.

- Simple techniques such as **4 + 1 Questions** can be helpful for reviewing progress and reframing.
- **Funnel** questions are a way to extract more details gradually.
- **Probing** questions help you gain detail and clarity. **5 Whys** is one example of ways to ask probing questions.
- **Leading** questions are a good technique if you're trying to persuade someone, but they can leave the other person feeling as if they have little or no choice.
- **Rhetorical** questions encourage reflection (but aren't really questions).

Open and closed questions

A closed question usually receives a single word or very short, factual answer. For example, 'Are you thirsty?' The answer is 'Yes' or 'No'; for 'Where do you live?', the answer is generally the name of your town or your address.

Open questions elicit longer answers. They usually begin with what, why and how. An open question asks the respondent for his or her knowledge, opinion or feelings. 'Tell me' and 'describe' can also be used in the same way as open questions. For example, tell me what happened next.

Open questions are good for:

- developing an open conversation: 'What did you like about your work experience?';
- finding out more details: 'What else do we need to do to make this happen?';
- finding out the other person's opinion or issues: 'What do you think about leaving school?'

Closed questions are good for:

- testing your understanding, or the other person's: 'So, if I get this qualification, I will get a job?'
- concluding a discussion or making a decision: 'Now we know what needs to be done, are we agreed this is the right course of action?'
- frame setting: 'Are you happy with your predicted grades?'

A misplaced closed question, on the other hand, can kill the conversation and lead to awkward silences, so it is best avoided when a conversation is in full flow.

4 +1 Questions

What it does

It can help people think about a particular challenge or situation and plan for change. Because the '4 plus 1' questions are answered by more than one person, it groups together learning from different perspectives.

How it helps

It can be used to update a one-page profile or to review a project or plan. It is a quick way to work out better ways of supporting people or working together.

Funnel questions

This technique involves starting with general questions and then drilling down to a more specific point in each. Usually, this will involve asking for more and more detail at each level.

Example:

'Did you go for an interview?' *'Yes'* 'Who did you meet?' *'Some staff.'* 'What were their jobs?' *'Mostly managers.'* 'Did any of them give you their job title or a contact email or phone number?' *'Yes, one of them did."* 'Who was that?' *'A chap called Sal who worked in the factory.'* 'Can you remember if you saved the contact details?' *'Now you come to mention it, yes, I remember putting it in my phone.'*

Using this technique, you can help someone to re-live an experience and to gradually focus on a useful detail. It is unlikely you would have gotten this information by simply asking an open question such as 'Are there any details you can give me about what you saw?'

Tip

When using funnel questioning, start with closed questions. As you progress through the funnel, start using more open questions.

Funnel questions are good for:

- finding out more details about a specific point: 'Tell me more about Sal.'
- gaining the interest or increasing the confidence of the person you're speaking with: 'Have you used the Helpdesk?', 'Did it solve your problem?', 'What was the attitude of the person who took your call?'

Probing questions

Asking probing questions is another strategy for finding out more detail. Sometimes it's as simple as asking your respondent for an example to help you understand a statement that they have made. At other times, you need additional information for clarification.

'When do you need this action plan by? And do you want to see a draught before I give you the final version?'

Or to investigate whether there is proof for what has been said, 'How do you know that the teacher won't help you?'

Tip
Use questions that include the word 'exactly' to probe further: 'What exactly do you mean by difficult?' or 'Who, exactly, wanted you to do this?'

Probing questions are good for:

- gaining clarification to ensure that you have the whole story and that you understand it thoroughly;
- drawing information out of people who are trying to avoid telling you something.

5 Whys
Getting to the Root of a Problem Quickly

An effective way of probing is to use the 5 Whys method, which can help you quickly get to the root of a problem.

- The 5 Whys technique is most effective when the answers come from people who have hands-on experience with the process or problem in question.
- The method is remarkably simple: when a problem occurs, you drill down to its root cause by asking 'Why?' five times. Then, when a countermeasure becomes apparent, you follow it through to prevent the issue from recurring.

The 5 Whys uses 'countermeasures' rather than 'solutions'.

A countermeasure is an action or set of actions that seeks to prevent the problem from arising again, while a solution may just seek to deal with the symptom. As such, countermeasures are more robust and will more likely prevent the problem from recurring.

Have you ever had a problem that refused to go away? For example, 'I keep making the same mistakes when I'm choosing things' or 'I never get anywhere on time.'

Stubborn or recurrent problems are often symptoms of deeper issues. 'Quick fixes' may seem convenient, but they often solve only the surface issues and waste resources that could otherwise be used to tackle the real cause.

When to use a 5 Whys analysis

You can use 5 Whys for troubleshooting, quality improvement and problem-solving, but it is most effective when used to resolve simpler problems. It is excellent for thinking about new strategies to try in action planning!

You'll know that you've revealed the root cause of a problem when asking 'why' produces no more useful responses, and you can go no further.

It may not be suitable if you need to tackle a complex or critical problem. This is because 5 Whys can lead you to pursue a single track, or a limited number of tracks, of inquiry when, in fact, there could be multiple causes.

Leading questions

Leading questions try to lead the respondent to your way of thinking. They can do this in several ways:

- **With an assumption** – 'How late do you think your project report will be?' This assumes that the project will certainly not be completed on time.
- **By adding a personal appeal to agree at the end** – 'Lori's very efficient, don't you think?' or 'Option Two is better, isn't it?'
- **Phrasing the question so that the 'easiest' response is 'yes'** – our natural tendency to prefer to say 'yes' than 'no' plays an important part in the phrasing of questions: 'Shall we think about your backup plan now?' is more likely to get a positive response than 'Do you want a backup plan or not?' A good way of doing this is to make it personal. For example, 'Would you like a backup plan?' rather than 'Shall we think about your backup plan?'
- **Giving people a choice between two options** – both of which you would be happy with – rather than the choice of one option or not doing anything at all. Strictly speaking, the choice of 'neither' is still available when you ask, 'Which would you prefer . . . A or B?', but most people will be caught up in deciding between your two preferences.

Note that leading questions tend to be closed.

Leading questions are good for:

- getting the answer you want;
- closing a sale: 'If that answers all of your questions, shall we agree on a price?'

Leading questions are not good when:

- they leave the other person feeling that they haven't had a real choice;
- you use them in a self-serving way or in one that harms the interests of the other person, then they can, quite rightly, be seen as manipulative and dishonest.

Not asking questions

Rhetorical questions

Rhetorical questions aren't really questions at all, in that they don't expect an answer. They're really just statements phrased in question form: 'Isn't that creative?' 'I wonder how you produce such a fabulous finish on the wood?' 'How on earth can people work that machine so quickly?'

People use rhetorical questions because they are engaging the listener rather than making them feel that they are being 'told' something or expected to reply.

Rhetorical questions are good for:

- when people are reluctant, or unable, to talk, for example, if someone has selective mutism;
- engaging the listener;
- allowing people time to reduce anxiety about having to answer questions.

Using description and narrative

Many questions can be difficult to answer without context.

When we ask people to 'describe' something, there is no right or wrong – it is their reality, so is often much easier as a response.

We can begin with *what?* rather than *why?* or *how?*

This offers context for further questions.

> *The single biggest problem in communication is the illusion that it has taken place.*
> ~George Bernard Shaw

Pre-session information

Pre-session information can be really useful in helping people understand what they should expect when meeting us.

- Add a photo of yourself so that people can see whom they will be meeting.

It can include a variety of things, such as how the session is delivered, by whom and how. You can find examples on the CXK website.

Written information can seem quite complicated, so you may want to try other approaches:

- a bespoke video for clients to watch before they come in. This tackles two aspects: one being a clear explanation of what we do and how we work, the other helping to reduce anxiety and worry that clients may face in meeting an unknown adult. Add subtitles, captions and transcripts for a more accessible resource!
- embed information on the organisation's website with a change in language to make things more inclusive;
- provide worksheets and/or infographics/posters which explain the service in a simplified manner to help prepare students;
- share information in group sessions prior to interventions – this not only gives people an opportunity to ask questions but also means that teaching staff hear the same messages;
- share information with circles of support.

> One of our schools provides a set of plasma-screen slides (which play as part of the loop on the screens in the school). These cover what we do, how we work and a fun fact for each adviser in the school. They are easy to make using PowerPoint software and very effective in not only promoting our services but also explaining what we do (demystifying 'careers').

The resources section has links to lots of further information and tools to add to your toolkit. You can access it via the QR code and URL at the start of the book.

For some explanations about different impairments, and some of the words and phrases used within learning support and disability communities, have a look at our glossary.

Chapter 3
'Disability'

Disability is part of being human.

Almost everyone will temporarily or permanently experience disability at some point in their life. Over one billion people – about 15% of the global population – live with some form of disability, and this number is increasing.

The **World Health Organization** defines Disability as an umbrella term covering:

- **Impairments**

issues with body function or structure;

- **Activity limitations**

difficulties in doing a task or action;

- **Participation restrictions**

difficulties experienced by a person when involved in life situations.

Disability thus reflects the complex interaction between features of:

- a person's body;
- the society in which he or she lives;

We should do all we reasonably can to create an environment where people feel safe and comfortable talking about disability. This can help towards:

- making disabled people aware that they have rights;
- making sure disabled people get any support they need and are not put at a disadvantage or treated less favourably;
- recognising the benefits of an inclusive and diverse learning and workforce that does not exclude disabled people;

- recruiting and retaining students and staff who bring skills they have learnt through living with a disability;
- avoiding situations where we are unaware that someone is disabled and feel negatively about them for not doing something; and
- improving wellbeing and productivity for everyone.

> **Some people don't like the word 'disability'**
>
> 'Dis', the prefix, means to be set apart a little bit, that you are over and above and beyond whatever is attached to that word.
>
> So . . . *dis*ability is beyond ability, reframing ability, putting ability in a new context, looking at it from a new angle, from a different direction.
>
> When young people leave education, they no longer have Special Educational Needs, Additional Support for Learning or Additional Learning Needs (which are the terms they will have become used to). To access support and funding in adult settings, they will often need to use the word 'disabled'.
>
> An alternative term to disabled is dif-able: differently able. When you become disabled, it's a trade-off, not a loss. You don't lose your abilities; they just change.

Models of Disability

Within the ***Medical Model*** of Disability, it is the failure or limitation of the individual's body that causes disadvantage. This suggests that the problem is with the disabled person. Use of words like *patient, case, tragedy, handicap, sufferer* to describe disabled people is symptomatic of the Medical Model of Disability.

Within the ***Social Model***, how an individual's body works doesn't matter because people are 'disabled' through lack of access to buildings, information, communication or personal support, or by the attitudes of others. It recognises that, from a disabled person's perspective, the problems they face are the barriers they experience in society rather than being 'disabled by a condition': we are disabled from achieving our potential because of the obstacles our non-inclusive society presents, not because we are physically unable.

In education and preparation for work settings (such as the job centre or supported employment), we tend to use a ***Charity model***. This model relies on others to fund services for people with a disability, rather than recognising personal support as a right. The Charity approach to disability is viewed as being in the 'best interests' of disabled people, but it does not consider disabled people's experiences and knowledge as necessarily valuable or essential.

The Spectrum Model asserts that disability does not necessarily mean a reduced spectrum of function.

An ***Identity (or Affirmation) Model*** is closely related to the social model of disability but with a difference in emphasis. It shares the social model's understanding that the experience of disability is socially constructed but differs to the extent that it claims disability as a positive identity.

- Get to know which models of disability are utilised by different organisations and services so that you can help your clients understand how they work and how to access the support they could offer.
- Funding and support are often based on a Charity model – we may need to support clients in clearly identifying the support they need. They may need to demonstrate what they require to achieve the same outcomes as their peers (e.g. *Access to Work*). Time to identify and try out support and strategies prior to transitions should be part of a career plan.
- Medical model: Support may require a diagnosis (e.g. *Disabled Student's Allowance*). Within the statutory schooling system, a diagnosis is usually not required; [identification of 'needs' are] so a client may need to plan in time to be diagnosed if Higher Education is something they are considering.

> ### Nothing about us without us
>
> The disability rights movement takes the position of 'no decision about me, without me'.
>
> If such a position is vital for the NHS, a national institution, surely the same should be said within careers work.
>
> We can see that this ethos has been carried over to the wider education community and other sectors.
>
> > *In the summer of 2023, the Pitt Williams Museum's Curating for Change Fellow, Kyle Lewis Jordan, led a group of co-producers in researching disability across multiple times and spaces. Their questions grew from asking how disabled people lived throughout time, to interrogating how the objects capture the experience of disability itself. Their ideas covered themes of Form and Function, Precarity and Violence, and Care.*
>
> Valerie Billingham in 1998 helped to advocate for patient inclusion with the phrase: 'Nothing about me without me.'
>
> If you are looking for a good read, try Mike Oliver's 'Social Model of Disability'.

The models adopted by educational settings can affect how support and discussions around next steps potentially develop for our clients.

The social model is congruent with our client-centred approach that places the client at the centre of our interactions and support.

An approach that builds upon and recognises the Social Model of Disability isn't a guarantee of success but is potentially one that is fairer and places the client at the centre of the work we do. It is a model we must listen to and attend to, especially as:

> The social model of disability is a way of thinking about disability, created by disabled people.

There is a risk that a client can be 'in the room' but still have decisions made about them, and for them, without their views being taken into consideration; this is considered being 'superficially inclusive'.

- *Chapter 11 looks in more depth at Mental Capacity, Advocacy and Equality Legislation in relation to our work.*

Career development professionals have a valuable role to play.

To ensure:

- the client's voice is heard and
- is given not just equal weight (to the professionals and family members in attendance), but is actively seen as being the most valuable.

It is vital that their voices and decisions are informed, which is where high-quality careers guidance comes in.

We are there to ensure that clients have the space for career support, time and support to understand the options and possibilities available to them, as well as explore what is important to them.

It is crucial that their career development professional has the tools, as well as the professional skills and training, to deliver the career guidance in a way that is accessible and inclusive; ensuring that it is not only meaningful but also worthwhile.

We hope this book goes some way towards supporting the development of those approaches and a toolkit.

How does disability affect decision-making?

Disabled young people are somewhat less likely to engage in certain risky behaviours than their non-disabled peers. They are also likely to have slightly smaller social networks.

What does this mean in terms of Career planning and decision-making?

Risk – many of us learn about managing risk through play (see Chapter 7 on Play theory), on the walk to work/school, by being in a sports team and by 'going out' with friends.

A lack of basic facilities, support and equipment prevents many disabled people from taking part in sport, social and play activities.

- We need to learn to manage risk and consequences in order to plan successfully.

Agency – many disabled young people are educated separately from their non-disabled peers (in special schools, alternative provision or specialist bases). They have limited choices about who they mix with, what they can do during their day and reduced access to the 'chatter' about future options which many of us experience.

- We need to practice making decisions and listening to alternative views in order to make effective decisions.

Location – our young people with learning support needs are often transported by taxi, sometimes to provision a long way from home. Friends tend to be based within their education setting, reducing opportunities for social interactions in their personal time. Many disabled adults say that they are lonely and isolated.

- We need to share our own thoughts and plans with people we trust to develop our own sense of the future.

> If your disabled clients have lacked opportunities to take risks, experience consequences, be heard, make choices, plan and build a wider circle of support, you may need to build these into their careers action plan.

The resources section has links to lots of further information and tools to add to your toolkit. You can access it via the QR code and URL at the start of the book.

For some explanations about different impairments, and some of the words and phrases used within learning support and disability communities, have a look at our glossary.

Chapter 4
Impairment and adjustments

The **public sector equality duty** (PSED) is a legal requirement for public authorities and organisations carrying out public functions. (Equality Act 2010)

Public authorities are organisations that work for, or provide services for, the public. For example, local councils, schools and education bodies, health providers, police, fire and transport providers, and government departments.

Organisations carrying out public functions are private businesses or volunteer organisations that are contracted to work on behalf of public authorities.

Equality law recognises that achieving equality for disabled people may mean changing the way that services are structured. This could be removing physical barriers or providing extra support for a disabled client.

This is the duty to make reasonable adjustments.

Making reasonable adjustments to Career Guidance

Every individual is different – so we cannot assume that an adjustment made for one person with a particular impairment will work for another with the same impairment, or that somebody with an impairment or health condition will consider themselves disabled by this.

- Do not make assumptions about an individual's ability to perform a task – ask, don't assume.

However, there are a range of things you can put in place which make it apparent that you can, and will, make reasonable adjustments.

Here are some ideas, and some reflections, to help you consider adjustments that could benefit you.

Engaging/relating to a person often involves chat or small talk – 'hello, how are you today?', 'nice weather', did you get here OK? and so on . . .

This may not make sense to some people and may take up a lot of energy!

An autistic young person's observations on 'chatting':

> 'Why do u [sic] think it's so exhausting chatting to people?' 'For a lot of us, it's exhausting because of what it involves . . . Listening to the other person and processing what they say, and then the energy required to formulate a response. If we are already low on spoons, then it just adds to the exhaustion we can experience' (National Autistic Society Community)[1]

- Remember to put any comments and questions you ask clients in context.

Planning – some people may need greater support for transition planning and implementing plans due to the nature of their disability. Helping them to make use of specific strategies that work for them and their condition(s) is crucial.

- Note: if co-occuring, it may be that strategies that work for other clients with non co-occuring conditions may cancel each other out. For example, this often happens with traditional coping or transition strategies used for autism and ADHD when they present together. Discussing with clients the strategies that have worked for them in the past is a useful way to help them identify strategies that will work for them now, as they plan their career transitions. For some clients that don't have a starting point for this and can feel lost, it might be that the first part of their plan is to help them identify (with support from home) the strategies that work for them (to lay the foundations of future success).

Co-occurance is when two or more, distinct conditions are present at the same time. They may exist together for many reasons, including shared causes and risk factors.

Making changes to the environment

Examples:

- Changing the lighting – some people are light sensitive. It costs nothing to ask if someone would prefer the light on or off.
- Changing the layout of a work area or the entrance to a building – don't wait until someone can't get in. Consider who might need access and furnish accordingly.

- Providing an accessible car parking space.
- Holding an interview in a room that's accessible for someone who uses a wheelchair or mobility aid, or brings a support worker with them – if you don't have one in your normal place of work find one elsewhere and have a plan in place for when you need it. Tell people in advance that you can provide it (and if they need to let you know prior to meeting).
- Offering a quiet, private room to meet in. This is ideal for all 1:1 interventions, but particularly important if we will be asking personal questions.
- Meeting in a different building, online or outdoors! Consider if your client needs to move around, struggles with travel or has anxiety related to new places or journeys. You can also send a video of the route from outside to where the individual will be meeting you.
- Ensure that toilets are accessible – just because it has a picture of a wheelchair on the door doesn't mean it will be accessible for everyone. You may have to consider proximity, room for an additional person or room to park a wheelchair and transfer.
- Providing information about your accessible facilities via your pre-session information, website or social media. Aim to include photographs and dimensions.
- Moving careers activities to a more accessible venue or offering them in a range of settings – for example, not everyone can engage in a large assembly (consider offering an alternative for those who can't so they don't miss out on the UCAS talk!)
- Providng a 'quiet or calm time' during a career fair where there are fewer people, less noise and the lights are dimmed.

Making changes to the format of support

Examples:

- Changing the time of a session – this may help if a person has medication in the morning, is uncomfortable on busy public transport, gets very tired at certain times of day. For example, open days at colleges and universities may be overwhelming for some people – ask the learning support team for an alternative time to visit.
- Splitting sessions into smaller chunks . . . can help with energy, focus and concentration.
- Additional pre-session information can be useful in reducing anxiety. Some people will feel better if they can SEE you before they meet you, so do add a photo. If you explain in advance that you are happy to make reasonable adjustments, it makes it easier for people to ask. There are some examples in Chapter 2.

- Offering visible choices – you can send examples prior to meeting, use cards or sticky notes for people to choose from or use a practical activity. Not everyone works best with words, so having a few strategies that involve movement or pictures and writing the words down can help.

- 'Just one thing' – we endeavour to provide clients with ALL their options and choices. When we are time constrained we often present these all at once. If someone struggles with information overload, start with just one thing and add in more later – say what you are doing so the client knows you are taking a gradual approach.
- Prompting ideas. Not everyone has the ability to 'imagine' their future self – making it impossible to answer questions like 'where do you see yourself in 5 years'. A good way to start from present self and work forward is 'Good Day, Bad Day'. There is a great template on the NDTi website.
- Revisiting the 'contract' regularly. As you move through the exploration part of guidance, people's needs and ideas change. This can be particularly apparent for people with an impairment who experience barriers and challenges not encountered by their non-disabled peers. So check back on your planned work with them regularly to see what has changed.
- Sending questions ahead of time.
- 4 + 1 Questions can help people to think about a particular challenge or situation and plan for change. Because the 4 + 1 Questions are answered by more than one person, it groups together learning from different perspectives. It can 'reframe' thinking about things that have not gone to plan.

Chapter 2 takes you through a range of questioning techniques that you can use to adapt to people's needs, explains how we all process sensory information differently and gives information about assisted communication.

- If you are working with a support worker who assists with a person's communication, include them in your contracting at the beginning of your session and send them the same pre-session information as the client.

Establish clearly that:

- you want them to help with communication between you and the client, but NOT to talk for them;
- they should not offer their own opinion unless requested to by the client; and
- they are bound by the same confidentiality agreement as yourself and the client.

Changes to how we provide information

Use, and explain, the words people will hear and read.

Skills	Data protection
Strengths	Person-centred
Apprenticeship	Advocacy
Work	CV
College	Application
Higher Education	Reasonable adjustments
Training	Disability confident
Induction	Access to Work
Supported internship	Disabled
Mental capacity	Confidentiality

Ideas for reflection:

- Do an 'audit' of your invitation process.
- Ask people about their experience of finding and entering your meeting place.
- Ask clients if there are things they would have liked explained differently.
- Did the explanation of what would happen match their experience?
- Did anything make them anxious or reluctant to talk to you?
- Could they see, hear, understand what was going on?

Action plans

- Send information in different formats (voice recording, video recording, pictures or symbols). Check with your client what they would find most useful.

- Get permission to send information to a person of their choosing in their circle of support. This can be helpful when a client struggles with an aspect of planning or research and will require support. The temptation is to do it for them . . . however, that won't develop their career planning skills. If they will be using a circle of support ongoing, they are the best people to help develop those skills.
- Changing the font, colour or size of print could make a huge difference if you are printing plans. ASK.
- Adding some clear space between sections of an action plan can help people who struggle to 'scan' words or keep their place in a document.

    ✔ Chapter 9 has more on action planning.

Tech solutions to planning challenges: there are lots of apps – many free – that people find useful. Here are just a few examples . . .

- To organise, co-ordinate, complete and share tasks: *Asana, Remember the Milk, Due, Evernote, Dropbox, Priority Matrix, RescueTime, Wunderlist, ColorNote.*
- Budgeting: *YNAB.*
- Always late? Navigation apps such as *Waze.*
- Help with passwords: *LastPass.*
- Calming down: *Headspace, Calm, Breathe2Relax, BOLD Tranquility, Yoga Nidra, Naturespace.*

And some that are more costly, but specifically made for disabled people or education support needs such as Brain in Hand.

If you are looking at a screen together, you can change your settings to offer an accessible experience. Apple, Chromebook and Microsoft all have information online showing how you can adapt your computer.

Have a look at CXK's YouTube Channel for an exploration of neurodiversity and inclusion from the perpective of 'lived expereince' including videos on:

- whiteboards;
- earbuds;
- authentic self;
- pomodoro technique.

A personal note from Chris:

> *I am very grateful to work for an organisation which understands my needs, as both a practitioner and manager where I use 'fidget devices' to keep myself on track and take regular breaks.*
> *All of this requires effort and commitment, as well as time.*

Speech

Speech refers to the sounds that people make with their vocal cords.

It is distinct from language, which refers to the words people know and use.

As careers practitioners we primarily use speech, language and listening to communicate. So, when speech is an issue our communication skills are challenged.

Knowing a little about what can affect speech helps us adjust our communication to meet individual need.

The development of speech is affected by hearing, muscle tone, facial shape differences and challenges with learning and memory. Some conditions such as epilepsy, neurological differences or autism can also complicate this development. Speech development is complex for many people with an impairment.

Look at our glossary for more information on different types of impairment.

When people lack the ability to make certain sounds or cannot co-ordinate the sounds in the required sentence, this is described as having 'articulation' difficulties.

Dyspraxia, also known as developmental co-ordination disorder (DCD), is a common disorder that affects movement and co-ordination.

Dysarthria is where you have difficulty speaking because the muscles you use for speech are weak. It can be caused by conditions that damage your brain or nerves and some medicines.

Dysphasia, also known as aphasia, is where you have difficulty understanding words or putting them together in a sentence.

Some individuals may not be able to speak at all in your setting (selective mutism), may stammer and stutter or make involuntary vocal sounds (tics).

If a person's speech and language production appear to be delayed or disordered in any way when compared to other people their age, this is called an *expressive* language difficulty.

Stammering is defined as 'an involuntary repetition, prolongation or block which interrupts the normal flow of speech'. It can affect anyone, but boys are more likely to stammer than girls.

There is no one cause of stammering; rather, it is the result of several different factors combining in an individual at the same time. These factors include physical, emotional and external influences upon a person.

Medical evidence also suggests that some people who stammer have a greater difficulty in co-ordinating the muscles used for speech.

Stammering is not caused by a person being anxious. However, a person who stammers may be more anxious than others when placed in certain speaking situations:

- Because expressing themselves can be more awkward, people may avoid situations because of their speech. This includes talking with us!
- Ignoring it (pretend it isn't happening, don't mention/discuss it), does not make it go away. Offer opportunity to discuss it and identify useful strategies as part of career planning.
- Provide an appropriate speech model by speaking slowly, pausing and using shorter and simpler sentences yourself.
- Do not advise the person to talk slowly/relax/take a deep breath as it implies the person is stammering because they are doing something wrong.

People who stammer are aware of it. Most prefer to be allowed to continue speaking without others completing the sentence on their behalf. Give them time to communicate.

Selective mutism

Selective mutism as a fear (*phobia*) of talking in selective situations or to certain people.

It can start at any age, but most often starts in early childhood. It affects about 1 in 140 young children. It's more common in girls and children who have recently migrated from their country of birth.

The main warning sign is the marked contrast in ability to engage with different people, characterised by a sudden stillness and frozen facial expression when they're expected to talk to someone who's outside their comfort zone.

They may avoid eye contact, or avoid any form of communication – spoken, written or gestured.

If they have a speech and language disorder or hearing problem, it can make speaking even more stressful.

Some people have difficulty processing sensory information – for more about this, look back at Chapter 2.

A misconception is that a person with selective mutism is controlling or manipulative or has autism. There's no relationship between selective mutism and autism, although you may have both.

When mutism occurs as a symptom of post-traumatic stress, it follows a very different pattern and the person suddenly stops talking in environments where they previously had no difficulty.

Non-verbal autism

Some autistic people are delayed in their use of language, and some don't use speech.

People may use a range of other techniques to communicate including Assistive Technology devices or picture-based communication boards; gestures; taking your hand to an object or reaching; looking at words or objects; echolalia (the repetition of other people's words); crying or distressed behaviour.

Assistive technology (AT) is any item, piece of equipment, software program or product system that is used to increase, maintain or improve functional capabilities.

Augmentative and Alternative Communication (AAC) refers to using communicative systems which augment a message and may be alternative to speech.

Effective use of AT and AAC can be empowering:

- Ask your clients to bring their AT/AAC aids with them when appointments are booked.
- Allow enough time in interventions.
- If you want to learn more . . . *Listen* is a short film in which nonspeaking autistic people talk about how nonspeakers are represented in books, theatre and film. They provide guidance for changing the narrative.

Tourette syndrome (TS) is a neurological condition characterised by repeated involuntary movements and uncontrollable vocal (phonic) sounds called tics. Sometimes tics can include inappropriate words and phrases.

Motor and vocal tics may make people reluctant to read aloud, ask or answer questions and even sometimes to ask for help. They may affect: communication, planning, time management, organisation and initiating tasks.

Hidden tics can also inhibit auditory processing. Such tics may include intrusive thought tics, visual tics and so on. These tics are usually internal and not obvious to see.

Cerebral palsy

Speech and communication difficulties are common in people who have cerebral palsy.

This can be due to a range of factors including difficulty with facial muscle control. Difficulties in communication may also be due to factors such as sensory issues and articulation problems.

Different types of cerebral palsy may bring different issues. For example, those with Hypertonic cerebral palsy may find that their speech sounds slow and oral movements may require a lot of effort.

Those with Ataxic cerebral palsy may notice that they have pauses in their speech and may also have problems with swallowing.

Down's syndrome

Speech is almost always delayed for people with Down's syndrome. It takes longer for them to learn to co-ordinate their speech muscles and develop the accuracy needed for speaking. Other speech differences you might notice include:

- Speech that is hard to understand.
- Completely missing sounds, for example, cannot say the 'k' sound in any context.
- Sounds missing in specific contexts, for example, they leave the last sound off words.
- Stuttering or other dysfluencies, for example, the words sound stuck or jumbled or repeated.
- They can imitate a word, but can't say it independently or on command.

Brain injury

Brain injury can cause communication difficulties by impairing the physical ability to speak and/or the ability to understand and express language.

D/deaf (see Chapter 2 to find out more about our ears)

Deaf children growing up with cochlear implants or hearing aids often develop voices that sound the same as a hearing person.

For a deaf person who doesn't have hearing, their speech might be described as having a monotone nature or sound throaty or guttural.

Signing to assist or replace speech:

Makaton uses symbols, signs and speech to enable people to communicate. It supports the development of communication skills such as attention and listening, comprehension, memory, recall and organisation of language and expression.

Signs are used, with speech, in spoken word order. This helps provide extra clues about what someone is saying. Using signs can help people who have no speech, or whose speech is unclear. Using symbols can help people who have limited speech and those who cannot, or prefer not to, sign.

Sign language

Sign Language is a visual means of communicating using gestures, facial expression and body language. Sign Language is used mainly by people who are D/deaf or have hearing impairments.

Many people think that sign language is a universal language used by all D/deaf people – this is not true!

British Sign Language (BSL) is the signed language of the D/deaf Community in the UK.

It is an official language of England, Wales and Scotland, has its own grammatical structure and syntax, and as a language it is not dependent, nor is it strongly related to, spoken English.

You can do BSL instead of English as part of an apprenticeship.

Northern Ireland has two signed languages – British Sign Language (BSL) and Irish Sign Language (ISL).

Finger spelling is used in sign language to spell out names of people and places for which there is not a sign. It can also be used to spell words for signs that the signer does not know the sign for, or to clarify a sign that is not known by the person reading the signer.

Sign Supported English is a method of communication that uses BSL signs, but the structure and grammar are based on spoken English. This means the signs follow the exact order they would be spoken in.

This variation of BSL doesn't require any knowledge of BSL grammar structure, so it is easier for hearing people to learn.

- It is estimated that 10% of all children have long-term or persistent speech, language and communication needs (SLCN).
- Some basic signs are common to Makaton and BSL, so it may be helpful for you to learn a few if you are frequently working with people who sign.
- You would need to sign to an incredibly high standard to conduct a full Career Guidance intervention, so ask about signing support if you are working with D/deaf people.

Don't assume someone has not got mental capacity just because they can't speak.

Note

1 https://community.autism.org.uk/f/miscellaneous-and-chat/34828/chit-chat

Chapter 5
Navigate the systems of support

There are a range of systems of support for disabled people going through education, training and work, and also many organisations that can help with looking for and securing work.

We can't mention all of them, but wanted to give an overview of the types of support available and how to get the support. Links to a range of support and organisations can be found in the resources section.

- Make sure people know there **is** support. It is not unusual for people to be anxious when they think their current support will end – if they know support is available in their next setting, they can add this to their career plan.
- Signpost to explainers on **how** to get support – going through the process of securing funding and/or support is often the hardest part.

Go to our glossary for an alphabetical list of the words and acronyms used within these education and support systems, with brief explanations of what they mean.

Support in learning

Scotland has an inclusive educational system which focuses on overcoming barriers to learning and Getting it Right for Every Child (GIRFEC).

By law, education authorities must identify, provide for and review the additional support needs of their pupils.

The Education (Additional Support for Learning) (Scotland) Act 2004 sets out the duties of education authorities and the rights of parents, children and young people to additional support for learning.

- *My Rights My Say* is a children's service supporting children aged 12–15 to use their rights. They provide advice and information, advocacy

support, legal representation and a service to independently seek children's views about the support they receive with their learning.
- Reach is a website dedicated to children and young people, aiming to help them feel supported, included, listened to and involved in decisions at school. It has information and advice for pupils about their rights to additional support for learning; practical tips for all sorts of school problems; young people's real-life stories; and positive examples of pupil participation.

'Additional support for learning' is the term used to describe any support that is extra or different from the help that most children receive. It can include help that is focused on learning and support to be fully involved in school life.

There are many types of support available, including:

- changes to the curriculum or the way a pupil is taught;
- support from a learning assistant;
- use of technology or changes to learning materials;
- input from specialist teachers or health professionals.

Co-ordinated Support Plans:

A CSP is a plan used for some pupils who need significant additional support with their learning. It is used to help professionals from different agencies to work together. A CSP should set out broad and long-term goals for a pupil's education. It should be reviewed at least every 12 months.

Wales

The Special Educational Needs (SEN) system in Wales is being replaced by the Additional Learning Needs (ALN) system.

This is happening over four school years, between September 2021 and August 2025.

During the four-year implementation period, the ALN system will operate alongside the SEN system.

All children with Additional Learning Needs will have an Individual Development Plan, which will replace the current SEN Statement, Individual Education Plan, or Learning and Skills Plan.

Learners with any level of Additional Learning Need who require Additional Learning Provision (ALP) to be made for them will be entitled to an IDP outlining their support needs. This new system will protect the rights of all children, regardless of the extent of their additional learning needs.

Any existing statements will continue to be legal documents until replaced by an IDP or until the local authority ends the statement.

The ALN system will replace the separate systems for special educational needs (SEN) and learning difficulties and/or disabilities (LDD) in further education to create a single system for supporting learners from 0 to 25 with ALN.

> Under the new Additional Learning Needs and Education Tribunal Act (ALNET) one of the key priorities for school Additional Learning Needs Co-ordinators (ALNCos) is to liaise with careers specialists to ensure that learners with ALN receive appropriate career guidance.

Organisations that can offer help and advice include:

- Careers Wales;
- SNAP Cymru;
- National Deaf Children's Society;
- National Autistic Society Cymru;
- Royal National Institute of Blind People (RNIB) Cymru;
- Children's Commissioner for Wales.

The Additional Learning Needs Code for Wales 2021 contains statutory guidance.

England

Special educational provision in schools is called SEN support.

If a school has taken relevant action to identify and meet needs, but expected progress is still not being made, then an Education, Health and Care needs assessment can be requested.

Education, Health and Care Plans (EHCPs) are for children and young people who need more support than their school or other setting can provide.

The plans can start from a child's birth and continue into further education and training (from 0 to 25).

All children in special schools should have an EHC plan setting out the provision required to meet their needs.

Special Needs Jungle has useful flow charts describing the processes of requesting and conducting an EHCP needs assessment.

Each Local Authority has a 'SEND Local Offer' which should include:

- provision in the local authority's area;
- provision outside the local area that the local authority expects is likely to be used by children and young people with SEN for whom they are responsible, and disabled children and young people;
- relevant regional and national specialist provision.

If a young person aged 16–19 has an EHC plan, funding or high needs funding can continue up to age 25.

If a student aged 19–25 does not have an EHC plan, they may still be eligible for funding under the ESFA Adult Education Budget Learning Support.

The local authority must not cease an EHC plan simply because a young person has reached 19 years of age. However, there is no automatic entitlement to education provision up to age 25.

A personal budget is a notional amount of money that would be needed to cover the cost of making the special educational provision specified in the EHC plan. You cannot have a personal budget unless you have an EHC plan. Information about the availability of personal budgets must be contained in the Local Authority's local offer.

A Local Authority is obliged to consider identifying a personal budget for educational provision only if it is requested when it issues a draft EHC plan following an EHC needs assessment or when it is reviewing an EHC plan.

Northern Ireland

The Department of Education (DE) and Education Authority (EA) are currently undertaking an end-to-end review of SEN.

At the time of writing: It is the school's decision to place a child on the SEN Register. Pupils with SEN may have more than one type of need. Children or young people not on the SEN Register have their learning needs met through whole-school educational provision, which includes differentiation and reasonable adjustments.

If a pupil has a medical need, this is recorded on the school's medical register. Schools will add a pupil to the medical register based on information provided by their parents or carers or from a Health and Social Care Trust (HSCT).

A pupil can be recorded on the SEN Register and the Medical Register if they have both a medical need and require special educational provision.

Stages of Special Educational Provision in the SEN Code:

Stage 1: School-Delivered Special Educational Provision;

Stage 2: School-Delivered Special Educational Provision plus External Provision;

Stage 3: Statement of SEN.

Colleges have a legal duty to try to meet the learning support needs of young people studying with them. Colleges can offer different kinds of support depending on students' needs. For example, the college might offer extra learning sessions, mental health support, occupational therapy or some technology to help the student. The college should involve the student when planning their support.

Specialist colleges provide post-16 education to young people with learning difficulties and/or disabilities when their needs cannot be met at a general further education college.

There are currently around 99 specialist colleges across England and Wales. In addition to both independent and state specialist colleges, some offer residential accommodation for students, with around-the-clock care.

The colleges have a holistic approach, providing physical and mental care as well as further education and training for their students.

Supported internships

Supported Internships are an educational study programme for young people with learning disabilities aged 16–24 with an Education, Health and Care Plan (EHCP), or their equivalents in Wales and Scotland, who want to move into employment and need extra support to do so.

Inclusive apprenticeships

Apprentices with an EHC plan or 'legacy statement' can now apply for an adjustment to the minimum standards of English and Maths required to an Entry Level 3. The training provider must provide evidence that, even with support, reasonable adjustments and 'stepping stone' qualifications, the apprentice has not achieved the minimum level of English or Maths because of their learning disability or difficulty.

British Sign Language can be an alternative to English Functional Skills for Deaf people whose first language is BSL.

Access to Work can be used for Supported Internships, Traineeships and Apprenticeships

Note: 'Young people who start a work placement with an employer as part of the Department for Education supported internship programme or a traineeship will be able to apply for Access to Work ... No other types of unpaid internships/traineeships will qualify' reference: https://www.gov.uk/government/publications/access-to-work-guide-for-employers/access-to-work-factsheet-for-employers

Higher education

Disabled Students Allowance (DSA)

What is DSA?

It is a grant that is provided by the government to pay for any additional study-related costs Higher Education students may have as a direct result of their disability.

- It is not a loan and does not need to be paid back.
- It is not means-tested or related to family income.

Who is it for?

Students (UK nationals) can apply for DSA if they have a disability that affects their ability to study, such as a:

- specific learning difficulty, for example, dyslexia or ADHD;
- mental health condition, for example, anxiety or depression;
- physical disability, for example, if they have to use crutches;
- a wheelchair or a special keyboard;
- sensory disability, for example, if they are visually impaired, deaf or have a hearing impairment;
- long-term health condition, for example, cancer, chronic heart disease or HIV.

They must:

- be an undergraduate or postgraduate student (including Open University or distance learning);
- qualify for student finance from all Student Finance services in the UK; and
- be studying in a course that lasts at least a year.

What support can people get through DSA?

DSA pays for four main categories of equipment and support, depending on individual requirements:

- Specialist equipment and software such as speech-to-text software, mind-mapping software, a digital voice recorder or ergonomic equipment.
- One-to-one support from a specialist support worker, such as a Study Skills Tutor (dyslexia tutor, for example), Specialist Mentor or BSL interpreter.
- A travel allowance to help with any additional travel costs.
- Support with additional study-related costs such as photocopying or printing materials.

People may not receive all of these elements of DSA. A Study Needs Assessment helps determine the most suitable support.

What evidence is needed?

- Disability or long-term health condition: A copy of a report or letter from a doctor/consultant or a disability evidence form via the Gov website.
- Mental health condition: A copy of a report or letter from a doctor or consultant.
- Specific learning difficulty such as dyslexia: A copy of a 'diagnostic assessment' from a practitioner psychologist or a suitably qualified specialist teacher.

When to apply?

Completing the DSA process can take up to 15 weeks.

- Apply for DSA from March before the academic year of study commences. For example, those starting university in September 2025 can apply for DSA from March 2025.
- Students do not need to wait until they have received exam results or have accepted their place at the university.
- DSA is a national process and will transfer between universities.
- Once awarded DSA, this will continue for the duration of their undergraduate course.

Where can you have an assessment?

- A DSA Hub or online Needs Assessment can be arranged. There is a useful video in the resources section about the DSA application process.
- The process varies depending on where in the UK people live.

Each of the home nations has its own application process and its own set of forms, although they are broadly similar. Use the links in the resources section to find the details for the area where your clients live.

Differences between school/FE and HE

School/FE

1. A diagnosis is not always required at school ('needs not label').
2. Exam arrangements may have been arranged through a Form 8 assessment.
3. Support is usually co-ordinated by a SENCo/ALNCo.
4. Parents, carers or guardians will have been involved in discussions on behalf of the student.

HE

1. The university will not know about your support needs unless you tell them – by sharing your disability.
2. Diagnostic evidence is required at university.
3. A Form 8 can be used for some adjustments, such as extra time in exams.
4. Support is co-ordinated by a Disability Adviser, within the Additional Learning Support or equivalent department (they are all called something slightly different!)
5. As an adult, the student must apply for funding and organise support themselves, with the help of Disability Services.
6. Support at university will look different from support at school.
7. Documentation related to statutory education (such as an EHCP, IDP or Statement) will end.

Support for job seekers

In the resources section we have put links to examples of organisations offering support to find work.

Many national and local charities offer this – some are specific to a type of impairment, and some are targeted at disabled people generally.

Please reach out to them. They offer amazing support and great opportunities.

Support ranges from peer mentoring to tailored disability-specific opportunities and information.

Many employers now see the value in employing disabled staff and use organisations like *Evenbreak, Diversity Jobs* and *Ambitious about Autism* to attract the candidates they don't engage with through standard recruitment processes.

This is just another form of networking! Work with your disabled clients and explore the benefits of approaching work opportunities from the 'disability as an asset' angle.

What other support is available?

Via the JobCentre, the **Work and Health Programme** offers personal support to a range of people who may face barriers to employment. Ask a Work Coach about eligibility.

There is a legal duty under the **Care Act 2014** to facilitate employment and volunteering opportunities for people with disabilities and other vulnerable adults. Ask a social worker for more information.

Access to Work is a government scheme designed to provide help to disabled people who have, or are applying for, a job and are experiencing disability-related challenges.

It applies to people living in England, Scotland and Wales. (Northern Ireland has an alternative)

It can be used for:

- Job coaching;
- Interpreters – preparing and having a communicator for interviews;
- Working interviews/job trials;
- Equipment, aids and apps;
- Signers;
- Disability awareness training;
- Job mentoring;
- Support workers;

- Travel training;
- Taxis; and
- Mental Health Support Service.

People can also access mental health support directly through Maximus.

Intensive Personalised Employment Support (IPES) is a provision aimed specifically at disabled people (as defined under the Equality Act 2010) with complex barriers to employment, for whom other support, such as the Work and Health Programme (WHP), is unsuitable. IPES is for clients who face complex barriers to employment and are considered by JobCentre Work Coaches to be more than 12 months from the labour market without intensive support.

Supported Employment is a personalised model for supporting disabled people to secure and retain paid employment. The model uses a partnership strategy to enable people to achieve sustainable long-term employment and businesses to employ workers.

Blind Person's Allowance is an extra amount of tax-free allowance.

If an employer displays the **'Disability Confident'** symbol this means:

- The employer is committed to employing disabled people.
- You'll be guaranteed an interview if you meet the basic conditions for the job.

Grants, bursaries and charitable organisations

Charities and grant-giving trusts rarely give money for things that the government provides for. There are search tools in the resources section to help people find organisations that give grants and to check their criteria.

There are also schemes – Education Maintenance Allowance (in Wales, Scotland and Northern Ireland) and Bursaries (in England) – for college students.

Transition from children's to adults' services

The legal age of becoming an adult within the care system is 16 years in Scotland but 18 years across England, Northern Ireland and Wales.

The age at which a child enters adult services will vary depending on where they live and their circumstances.

Legislation – different in each part of the UK – says that if a child, young carer or an adult caring for a child is likely to have needs when the child reaches adulthood, the local authority must assess them if it considers there is 'significant benefit' to the individual in doing so. This is regardless of whether the child or individual currently receives any services.

Some children will access aspects of adult health care before they are 18, while others may still be supported by children's services after their 18th birthday.

Transition in the healthcare system is often referred to as **NHS Continuing Healthcare**.

This is different from the social care system that is run by social services.

In Scotland, NHS Continuing Healthcare is called Hospital-Based Complex Care.

Health and Social Care services can give personal budgets or direct payments to people to pay for the support they need.

- As careers practitioners, we are not expected to know all the details about health and social care. However, being aware of processes, funding and support can help inform the careers and transition plans we form with our disabled clients.

Chapter 6
Ethics and agendas

Impartiality and transparency

As career development professionals, we have codes of ethics to guide and support us. When so many career practitioners are working in isolation, or for employers who may or may not buy into the ethical foundations of those who work within careers, having a safe haven to call our own is crucial.

Career development professionals have two main professional bodies, the CDI and AGCAS; individuals may be members of one or both. Each has an ethical code.

At their core are the principles of trustworthiness, transparency and impartiality.

Total impartiality isn't possible.

Bill Law summarises, in response to an article by Chris:

> *What might be called a 'client-centred' focus reflects the way a student or client talks about what's going on . . . while an 'expertise-informed' focus is on the information and diagnosis that a helper brings to that conversation. There's no necessary contradiction here. But the author wonders how much of it can be impartial.*

Due to this, how we handle this understanding is important. All of us will ask different questions of the clients we work with, due to our individuality. The nuances within the training and development we have each undertaken, and what we each see as being important within careers work, will affect what we explore and how we fulfil our roles as professionals.

Having self-awareness of where the questions we ask our clients come from is vitally important and can be found via the process of reflective practice.

Reflective practice

Reflective practice is the foundation of professional development; it makes meaning from experience and transforms insights into practical strategies for personal growth and professional impact.

It means:

- learning to pay attention;
- coming face to face with our assumptions;
- noticing patterns;
- changing what we see;
- changing the way we see.

How do we become a reflective practitioner?

- develop the skill of critically reflecting on experiences;
- improve your ability to think on your feet;
- combine insight with intention to apply learning in professional life.

There are four stages to this process:

Re-inhabit (relive the experience);
Reflect (notice what is going on);
Review (critically analyse the situation);
Reframe (capture new understanding).

Things to do that will help reflection:

- Notice patterns of thoughts, feelings and physical responses as they happen, and use this information to choose what to do.
- Give yourself time – the most often cited reason why we skimp on reflective practice is a lack of time. Build reflective time into your schedule.
- Allow yourself to pay attention – minimise distractions.
- Adapt your pace to enable reflection – slow down.
- Be curious – approach your reflective practice without judgement or self-criticism. There is no 'right way' to do this.
- Experiment!

Why is reflective practice good for us and our clients?

A structure in the brain called the corpus callosum plays an important part in performance.

The corpus callosum is a thick band of nerve fibres that connects the left and right sides of the brain, transferring information between the brain hemispheres. It is true that the two hemispheres have locations involved with different functions, that is, within the left side of the brain, there is a dominance in analytical thinking, language processing and drawing on existing knowledge to solve problems, while within the right side of the brain, there is more of an association with intuition, creativity and understanding through metaphor and visualisation. However, we shouldn't be thinking we are more left or right brained as we are all **whole** brained and need processing to occur in both hemispheres. Reflective practice:

- can help revisit and strengthen the neuronal connections we need to develop new habits, skills and mindsets;
- has huge benefits in increasing self-awareness, which is a key component of emotional intelligence, and in developing a better understanding of others;
- can help you develop creative thinking skills; and
- encourages active engagement in work processes.

Dialogue

To develop our practice, we need to use both personal reflection and reflective dialogue with others.

The principles of dialogue are:

- listening to understand others rather than planning what you're going to say;
- suspending judgement and criticism;
- voicing, or speaking in the first person rather than abstractly; and
- respecting the views of others and their right to hold them.

A dialogue can be used as a way of exploring experiences, planning future actions and enabling participants to benefit from others' insights into their personal challenges.

- This is of particular use when we are working with people whose experiences are outside our own.

Once we each understand our drivers, and perhaps the ethical positions which influence our practice, we can check ourselves for conscious, and unconscious, bias.

To be as impartial as possible requires:

- transparency in our practice;
- seeking clarity within communication;
- stating explicitly why we ask the questions we do;
- reflection on bias and emotional responses; and
- empowering clients with a greater sense of agency and control.

Work should be done with, rather than to, our clients, rooting our practice in its client-centred foundations.

To support practitioners with this, Chris and some colleagues developed the Open Partnership Model (OPM) to provide a structured way to support practitioners to disclose their agendas, whether implicit or explicit. Do check it out – links are in the resources section.

The CDI Code of Ethics states:

Impartiality

Members will maintain awareness of any limitations on their impartiality, acknowledge potential impact and take a neutral and non-directive approach when working with clients. Where impartiality is not possible, members will declare this to the client promptly.

Transparency

Members will agree on the purpose and approach to their career development services and activities in an open and transparent manner to gain trust and informed consent.

The ACGAS Code of Ethics is similar:

Impartiality – embedding the principle of impartiality into the design and delivery of career development services so that students and graduates have the freedom to develop their own career paths. Any conflicts of interest will be declared as soon as they are known.

The Open Partnership Model and the above understanding of what impartiality is and isn't push us to be open and transparent, as well as declare to the client at the outset the extent to which we are impartial.

This could mean saying to clients, 'Although I won't tell you what to do, I will ask questions so you don't miss out on opportunities. Is this ok with you?'

As careers practitioners we are tasked with widening aspirations and raising awareness of opportunities so that clients don't miss out.

When contracting with a client – establishing the nature and purpose of the intervention – we can cover this as part of our ethical practice.

- It is important that all clients understand the purpose of our work. Try not to rush explanations. Give people time to process and to ask any questions about why we do what we do.

Careers guidance can also be seen in a social justice context.

> *I'm not necessarily saying that every organisation which does something that students, or careers professionals, disagree with should be no platformed, but I am saying that where we encounter moral and political issues that are important to our students and to our wider professional values, we do need to do something. . . . e.g. informing students about these issues, encouraging them to ask critical questions and so on. (Tristram Hooley)*

> *AGCAS supports the intention for students to hold conversations around sustainability and making their own choices. However, we are required to protect freedom of speech and do not encourage 'no platforming' of particular employers. A blanket ban on particular industry sector lacks nuance and does not take into account the careers within these sectors which are linked to transition to more sustainable industries (for example, decommissioning and cleanup). (ACGAS)*

> *There is a school of thought that contends that careers professionals should be promoting social justice and equality. I would argue that social justice and equity needs to include a consideration of the environment when making career decisions. It may be challenging for advisers who are used to working in a client-centred way. It could be argued that by pushing this issue we are being more directive than we are used to or believe we should be. But do we have a duty to do this? (David Roe)*

The issues are nuanced, with all of the above having their own 'agenda' and a position with regard to what careers practitioners and services should or shouldn't do.

Think about social justice in the context of our work with, and for, disabled people:

- Have you ever had young people with learning support needs not given an appointment with you because their teacher deemed it unnecessary?

- How often do we get told that numerous career paths are 'not realistic' for disabled people?
- Why is disability awareness and inclusive practice not a mandated part of our core training?
- Should we take others to task about these things?
- Should we encourage clients to challenge discrimination?

All of this comes down to ethics. Ethics are derived from debate, discussion and dialogue; as we can see from the impassioned writing and differing views above, they form the core of our identity as career development professionals. However, it is our professional ethics that contain and keep our personal views and values in check. Whether the professional ethics we abide by should change or not is a much larger discussion. Yet the differences in views are why being open and transparent with our clients with regards how we work, is just as important as the work we do. Clients can then make an informed choice as to whether they wish to work with us or not.

Despite the impossibility of being truly impartial, it remains a noble goal to pursue and orient ourselves by. Otherwise, who will decide what 'agendas' or causes are the ones to be pursued within practice?

Inclusivity within ethics

So why did we start our section on ethics by discussing transparency and impartiality?

- to provide real examples of how awareness of our ethical duties directly affects the choices we make in our day-to-day practice;
- to highlight the ethical conundrums we have to grapple with as practitioners.

Weighing up what we do, and what we have done, in our practice, reflecting and returning to what we do each day, is part of what makes us professionals. It isn't something that is 'policed' or 'monitored' and is something that only each of us can know whether we attend to on a regular basis.

With regard to 'inclusive careers guidance', it is just as important as the other ethical frameworks that affect our practice. Both the CDI and AGCAS take a position with regard to inclusivity within careers practice that is often at risk of being overlooked.

The CDI states:

Equity, Diversity and Inclusion:

Members will actively promote equity and diversity and work towards the removal of barriers to personal achievement resulting from prejudice, stereotyping and discrimination. Members will promote access to career development activities and services in a range of ways that are appropriate and ensure inclusion for all.

AGCAS states:

Members will adhere to the following core principles and standards of professional practice:

Equity and diversity – design, delivery and promotion of accessible services to meet the needs of all, irrespective of their age, disability, gender identity, race (including colour, nationality and ethnic or national origin), political or religious beliefs, and sexual orientation.

We love the fact that both professional bodies recognise we need to ensure activities are delivered in a range of ways that ensure inclusion. Yet how many of us have reviewed our resources or practice to ensure that this is the case?

- What can you do to ensure your practice is inclusive and in line with these ethics (from the resources you use to the environment in which you deliver careers guidance)?
- To what extent do you make assumptions about what each client can cope with and/or requires?
- To what extent do you check with each client and make changes as required?

Remember, context is everything, and what might work with one client doesn't with another. The extent to which you can manage and adjust the environment, resources and how you deliver services within your given organisational and contractual constraints will make your practice more (or less) inclusive.

Here are some suggestions that can promote more inclusive practices:

- Ask for a pen profile from schools or colleges for all the students before you see them, to include communication and pastoral needs (not just for those students with medically recognised additional needs or disabilities).
- Work with your delivery settings to help them develop inclusive habits and to make time for this.

- Ensure clients are told in advance of their career sessions and sent pre-session information.
- Base the room from which you provide careers guidance in a place which is accessible for all clients and practitioners.
- Consider the environment: background noise, light levels and smells, for example, is there passing traffic noise or smells? Is the light white or warm; is there a way to adjust the light levels?
- Be mindful of things which can trigger allergies such as plants with pollen. If there are plants (which are useful for oxygenating spaces), consider providing plants which are less likely to trigger allergies, for example, succulents, spider plants.
- Consider the pens you use. Are they toxic or smelly?
- If you are housed in a room which isn't appropriate, have you taken the time to advocate for the needs of your clients and yourself; work with your setting, and your manager, to seek better accommodation.
- Consider providing different formats for action plans (with agreement from the setting you are working in) to build in choice for your clients.
- Listen to the client's own language for clues as to how they relate to the world; do they 'see' the future or 'think' rather than 'feel' about their options? This can provide a huge insight into the language you can use which takes into account how they consider the world around them.

Clients with Autistic Spectrum Conditions (ASC) will use and understand 'feeling' words – contrary to the myth that people with ASC have an inability to 'feel' or empathise. It is worth noting that some feel very intensely and this can be a barrier to engaging with the world. See Chapter 7 for a case study looking at working with someone with a Pathological Demand Avoidance profile.

Ask, don't assume:

- How does your client prefer to process or access information: via pictures, diagrams or interactive tools? Books or on a screen?
- What format would your client like their action plan in?
- How much writing is too much when composing action plans?
- What font size, font colour and background colour would they like their action plan in?
- How many actions are realistic for them (rather than you)?
- Do they NEED a back-up plan?
- How do you help prepare clients for interviews? Does it work?
- Do you explore differentiated interview approaches and how to navigate these?

- How do clients know about the support available to them, and how they can prepare and advocate for themselves in the job market later?
- To what extent do you make assumptions about their needs?
- Do you ask each client how their needs manifest for them? (Remember, two different clients who have identical diagnoses can present completely differently.)
- When was the last time you asked your clients to provide you with feedback on your action plans as part of quality assurance and improving the service you offer?

All the above take time to form as both a habit in your practice and to deliver, which is why (for most clients) having access to a full careers session of at least 45 minutes is crucial to not only explore their needs but to also have their needs met while doing so.

A careers guidance interview is an impartial, one-to-one meeting between yourself and a professionally qualified careers adviser. A guidance interview can last about 45 minutes. A careers guidance interview is not like a job interview – there are no right or wrong answers. (NI Direct)

Common challenges

- **Forcing clients to have a back-up plan**

Many practitioners assume 'best practice' is that all clients need a back-up plan. This goes back to the 'agenda' of careers work and being transparent with regards our practice.

If we have a service offer which is funded via a provider or contract and asks that we ensure that clients have a 'back-up plan', then this needs to be declared at the start with our clients.

Provide choice – some clients actively don't want a back-up plan and may need to consider whether they wish to work with us if we cannot offer this choice. If we are independent of such a caveat in our careers work, then we need to be mindful of this built-in assumption that all clients 'need' a back-up plan.

The athlete and the careers plan:

While working with Year 11 students, helping them to explore their post-16 choices and options, Chris was working with an athlete who was aiming to apply for A-levels alongside their chosen sport. They had found a school with a decent sports academy programme, and sports scholarship, which they wanted to join.

He asked them how they felt about applying to more than one place, in case they didn't get in (so they had a back-up).

They then raised a point which changed Chris's approach to guidance.

They said, 'Sir, if I have a back-up I know I will fail.'

Chris asked what they meant by this.

'As an athlete, I focus on winning. Whenever I've had a choice that gives me a back-up or safety-net, I don't work as hard and rely on the safety-net catching me . . . I don't reach my goal.'

(Wow! thought Chris)

They went on to say . . . 'If I focus on my goal, I work harder and I am more likely to achieve.'

This was a student who knew themselves well, including what they needed to succeed.

So no back-up applications – just an offer that if they got stuck on results day they could call Chris.

They went on to achieve the grades and got a place in the sixth form with the sports academy programme.

Sometimes we learn as much from our clients as they gain from having us around to support them.

If you are looking at the pros and cons of back-up plans you could use metaphor to explain what they do:

Thanks go to the previous client (the athlete) for this concept!

- Imagine you are on a tightrope.
- Some people like the idea of a safety-net underneath them so, if something goes wrong, they will have something to catch them (a back-up).
- Others thrive without the safety-net, so they put all their effort into getting to their goal.
- What are your thoughts? How do you feel? What do you need to succeed?

Ethics and Agendas

Promotion of formal learning over other pathways

An assumption by many is that young people must remain in education, training or volunteering with training until they are 18.

Current guidance [Autumn 2024] states:

Scotland
If you turn 16 between 1 March and 30 September you can leave school after 31 May of that year.

If you turn 16 between 1 October and the end of February you can leave at the start of the Christmas holidays in that school year.

Wales
You can leave school on the last Friday in June, as long as you'll be 16 by the end of that school year's summer holidays.

Northern Ireland
If you turn 16 during the school year (between 1 September and 1 July) you can leave school after 30 June.

If you turn 16 between 2 July and 31 August you can't leave school until 30 June the following year.

England

You can leave school on the last Friday in June if you'll be 16 by the end of the summer holidays.

You must then do one of the following until you're 18:

- stay in full-time education, for example, at a college;
- start an apprenticeship;
- spend 20 hours or more a week working or volunteering, while in part-time education or training.

Statutory guidance is predominantly aimed at Local Authority and education staff – 'encouraging' young people to stay in education or training.

- What is our ethical duty as careers practitioners if we are employed by a local authority? Is it to declare our agenda on this matter?

The statutory guidance is also where schools and colleges in England are directed to secure Independent Career Guidance:

All maintained schools and academies are under a duty to secure independent careers guidance for pupils in years 7-13. This should be presented in an impartial manner and include information on the full range of education and training options, including apprenticeships. An equivalent requirement is included in funding agreements for further education colleges and sixth form colleges and applies to all students up to and including the age of 18 and 19-25 year olds with an EHC plan.

Participation of young people in education, employment or training Statutory guidance for local authorities as on April 2024:

- It is not the law that young people have to stay in full-time learning! And certainly not in the school they currently attend.
- We must remain sensitive to how some may interpret our responses, as well as how we provide information.
- Being explicit can be helpful in empowering clients to seize their future and make informed choices.

Does your education setting or funding authority have its own agenda?

- Some schools want more students in the sixth form.
- Some staff may feel staying at school is a 'better option' for a young person.
- Funding may vary for different options and funders may look first at the cheaper options.

Scenario

Head teacher: 'We aren't getting enough Year 11 students applying to our 6th Form. You need to encourage more to apply to us.'

CDP: 'I am duty bound, by my code of ethics, to remain neutral.'

Head: 'Hmmph'

CDP: 'I can't tell you why individual clients are applying elsewhere, due to our code of conduct with regards confidentiality, but I can provide you with some broad information and observations regards trends I am seeing with your cohort.'

- Option blocks were creating clashes with Sport, Health & Social and the Sciences. Students couldn't choose either of the former with the Sciences they wanted to study which meant many of the students who were considering Sports Science, Physiotherapy, Nursing and Midwifery were applying to a neighbouring sixth Form instead.
- The head consulted with the CDP regarding proposed option blocks for the forthcoming academic year (before they were set) for Year 9 GCSE choices and post-16.

Parents have agendas too.

Scenario:

Parent (complaint): 'Why did your adviser tell my son to go to college? Just because he's disabled does not mean he can't go to sixth form like the other students.'

CDP manager's response:

- Listening to the full complaint
- Explanation to the parent about our role (including that we explore all options with all clients)
- (Once the parent was satisfied about the nature of the guidance) Questions about what we needed to do to explain better to clients, and their circles of support, what we do; and where their views about disability, sixth form and college had come from
- Feedback of all kinds informs practice. Never underestimate the benefits of a good complaint!

Re-inhabit – let people tell their story before giving your own viewpoint.

Reflect – notice what was going on for you, the client and their circle of support.

Review – critically analyse the situation.

Reframe – capture new understanding.

Scenario:

The two students and the careers adviser

Students who the school said were at risk of being Not In Education Employment or Training (NEET).

Student 1 asked: 'Why the f##k they should listen to a Careers Adviser?' They were suspicious and wary of any agenda.

CDP explained what they did and how they worked.

The astute student 1 asked: 'Is it true that I must stay in school, go to college, volunteer or do an apprenticeship?'

CDP said: 'no' – student was clearly surprised at the response!

CDP:

- explained that Raising of the Participation Age (RPA) remains non-sanctionable, the government retains the right to introduce sanctions for parents or carers if they see fit but none so far had done so;
- didn't try to 'sell' anything and just stuck to the facts;
- went onto explain why the government believed RPA was important, that the evidence showed that those who stayed on in education or training or volunteering with training had greater life chances;
- went on to have a really good session with student 1 and explored lots of ideas.

Student 1 from the 'traveller community'. Exploration included a respectful discussion of how opportunities were changing and the challenges their family had faced in recent years.

Personal experiences of working in construction were shared and noted – for example, the sector has changed over the years, with more trained trades people and fewer labourers.

Later that day . . .

Student 1 returned with another student in tow: 'This is my cousin, I told them you were decent and that they could trust you. Could you have a chat with them as well?'

P.S. Student 1 went to college after Year 11 with a big part of the reason why, being that they had chosen this for themselves.

Not trying to sell anything, lie or fabricate when challenged earned not only their trust but that of the wider community too.

10-minute sessions

Some learning providers feel it suitable to provide 10-minute-long sessions which many people have commented upon as not being sufficient for careers guidance – 45 minutes being the recommended length for a session, by the CDI.

- What becomes the cut-off to what is deemed sufficient or insufficient when being client centred?

We could argue that several half-an-hour sessions, for the client with ADHD and who struggles to sit still, creates an inclusive environment for some of our clients to receive careers guidance. So, how about lots of shorter 10- or 15-minute sessions?

Who is to decide? Context, as always matters.

There is a big difference between a service which sees 25 or 30 students a day for '10-minute career sessions' without recourse for follow-up and one which is using 10-minute sessions as part of a triage process for later work, or to meet the needs of students with highly complex needs.

- The ethical dilemma, and the extent to which each careers practitioner can ask themselves whether they are delivering a client-centred service, is important to consider.

Bias and discrimination

Being aware of bias is crucial, especially with people or organisations looking to promote their own agenda.

The interconnected nature of social categorisations, such as disability, race, class and gender as they apply to a given individual or group, can create overlapping and interdependent systems of discrimination or disadvantage.

Intersectionality acknowledges that everyone has multiple identities and is subject to various forms of intersecting oppression. The term 'intersectionality' was first coined by civil rights scholar and the founding voice behind critical race theory, Kimberlé Crenshaw.

- Intersectionality is a lens to help us think about how individuals in the Disabled community experience disability discrimination differently depending on the additional social groups they belong to.

Ableism is the discrimination and social prejudice against disabled people based on the belief that 'typical' abilities are superior. It is rooted in the medical model of disability. It defines people by their disability.

Like racism and sexism, ableism classifies entire groups of people as 'less than' and includes harmful stereotypes, misconceptions and generalisations of people.

Be aware that this is not always a conscious agenda. Consider if you, or your colleagues, do any of these things:

- choosing an inaccessible venue for a meeting therefore excluding some participants;
- using someone's mobility device as a hand or footrest;
- framing disability as either tragic or inspirational;
- using a non-disabled person to play a disabled character in a photo or video;
- making a video that doesn't have audio description or closed captioning;
- using the accessible toilet when you are able to use the non-accessible one without pain or risk of injury;
- wearing scented products in a scent-free environment;
- talking to a disabled person like they are a child, talking about them instead of directly to them, or speaking for them;
- asking invasive questions about the medical history or personal life of a disabled person;
- assuming people have to have a visible disability to actually be disabled;
- questioning if someone is 'actually' disabled, or 'how much' they are disabled;
- asking, 'How did you become disabled?'

What are ablest micro-aggressions?

Micro-aggressions are everyday verbal or behavioural expressions that communicate a negative slight or insult in relation to someone's gender identity, race, sex, disability and so on.

Ableist micro-aggressions:

- 'That's lame.'
- 'You are so retarded.'
- 'That guy is crazy.'
- 'You're acting so bi-polar today.'
- 'Are you off your meds?'

- 'It's like the blind leading the blind.'
- 'My ideas fell on deaf ears.'
- 'She's a psycho.'
- 'I'm super OCD about how I clean my apartment.'
- 'Can I pray for you?'
- 'I don't think of you as disabled.'
- We are all thoughtless with words and actions so don't be too harsh on yourself. However, when you do catch yourself – or colleagues – doing or saying something ableist acknowledge it, discuss it, reflect on it and do something different next time.

Government agendas

These affect everything from education, national services, local government funding for particular schemes to how Job Centre and back-to-work programmes function.

Political agendas from the civil service and government affect the direction Careers Services take. It has been this way over the years, with each scheme having different parameters through which to measure success.

For a history of the various ways used to measure the 'success' of different agendas and career programmes (as well as how these had changed), try watching Chris' interview with Malcolm Scott or have a read of Michelle Stewart's recent book on the history of career services which provides an illuminating understanding of these changing services.

We write this book in the context of a new Labour government and news that National Careers Services in England may merge with Job Centre Plus in England; we have no idea how this will manifest, nor what agendas will be pursued. Time will tell!

Scotland, Wales and Northern Ireland have their own devolved governments and therefore different systems of careers support. While we are not going to dissect the pros and cons of each service, what is obvious is that the vagaries of each affect the extent to which an inclusive service can be offered.

State-funded systems and processes affect what is possible, from the agendas at play to the Management Information Systems in use. Careers development professionals have to work within the parameters provided by their respective services and whoever funds these; this can wildly affect what is possible and what adjustments can be applied or negotiated.

Governments and Local Authorities equally have their own agendas on Disability and Special Educational Needs. Year on year overspending on SEND budgets is having significant impact on the choices made available for children and young people with learning support needs. Soaring DWP spending is having a similar impact on disabled adults.

How does this impact on career development professionals?

When Local Authorities and Government Departments cut costs, they inevitably cut services, support and, ultimately, opportunities.

You may:

- be criticised for making people aware of 'high-cost' provision or support;
- find that your clients are not given actual choices;
- be told to only share limited options with clients.

Understanding Legislation, and our professional ethical codes, really helps here to explain to others why we are committed to giving impartial, independent Information, Advice and Guidance.

Education agendas

Our education system encompasses a wide range of systems and establishments: local government-maintained schools, academies and multi-academy trusts (MATs), private education, independent specialist providers, alternative provision, home education, Further Education colleges, sixth forms, universities, prisons, hospitals and so on.

Their agendas teach our young people how to think and respond. And this will affect how they approach career planning.

Consider the approaches used in your settings and reflect on the impact this may have on learners:

- What are their isolation, detention and exclusion policies?
- Do they use 'restraint'?
- Are they trying to 'keep' students in their provision (sixth form, another year of FE)?
- Do they send people they would like to leave to see the careers adviser?
- Do learners have freedom of movement and expression, or do they use a SLANT approach?

SLANT

Sit up, **L**ean forward, **A**nswer questions, **N**od your head and **T**rack the teacher.

No speaking in corridors between classes, and no toilet breaks during lessons – unless you have a pass due to having 'a specific medical need'.

Whether you are employed directly by an education provider, an external careers organisation or as an independent can affect what is possible and the extent you can challenge or influence the agendas pursued.

Keeping ethics at the centre of what we do is crucial to protect us, and our clients, from external agendas.

We must remain mindful that just because we are asked to prioritise an institution's agenda, it doesn't necessarily mean it is the right one or client centred. It's a challenge!

Working with our settings to develop inclusive client-centred approaches from the ground up can be a way to steer, challenge and redirect cultures. Sometimes, educational agendas which don't match our viewpoint come from different pedagogical viewpoints.

Pedagogy is the theory and practice of learning.

- Engaging in dialogue, and continuous professional development, with fellow education staff and senior leadership teams can be a way to help our approaches be better understood and accepted. Things don't always have to be a fight. Informed, diplomatic, approaches often succeed.

Funding

How Career Guidance is funded can have a huge effect with regards how inclusive a service is and the extent to which the basics are delivered: such as the number of appointments which are available to clients, the length of appointments, time for follow-up work and ongoing support, as well as the resources available to you.

It is all well and good us writing about useful card decks and web tools to use, but if a service can't afford these, due to lack of funding and/or context, this limits what is possible.

- We have tried to highlight as many free and Do-It-Yourself resources as possible to help those of us who are economically challenged.

We know of schools and colleges in England who believe in doing the best for their young people but, due to lack of funding, can only afford one careers guidance session per student regardless of need. Funding in Scotland, Wales and Northern Ireland is centralised and offers more consistency.

Many young people who have additional needs become electively home educated or pursue EOTAS (Education Other Than At School) or Alternative Provision (AP) when other settings struggle to meet their needs. The onus for funding Careers Guidance in England is put on schools, colleges and universities – so on whose agenda are the careers of young people out of school?

Funding to support individuals can also make a huge difference.

- Become familiar with sources of funding which you can signpost to. We have highlighted some of these in Chapter 5 and in the resources section.
- Develop some links with the post-16 learning support and funding teams to help access intelligence on localised funding rules and agreements which, in turn, help us to support our young people.

Media

How many media stories contain the bit about how 'my careers adviser told me I would never succeed'?

And how many explain what we ACTUALLY do?

Yes, we get bad press. Often because our clients don't know who is a properly qualified professional and who is simply someone with 'Careers' in their job title giving them an opinion.

- The more people who understand the difference, the less this will happen. So let's tell our clients, their educators, their circles of support what we ACTUALLY do.

The media also often portray disabled people as either objects of pity or superhuman.

And sometimes they put the two together to explain how careers advisers dismiss the potential of disabled people!

The article in the *Guardian* about Jason Arday – *'he learned to talk at 11 and read at 18 – then became Cambridge's youngest Black professor'* – is an interesting read and a good illustration.

The resources section has links to the articles and books cited, plus lots of further information, explainers and tools to add to your toolkit. You can access it via the QR code and URL at the start of the book.

Chapter 7
Creating individualised approaches

In this chapter, we look at HOW we can deliver guidance in an individualised way.

Have a look at the resources section for more information and useful links.

Self

Activities that can promote the development of self-awareness:

- Mind clouds – where clients map out in clouds or bubbles what is important to them and/or the skills they have to navigate the future.
- Self-portraits – clients can create a portrait that shows how they feel about the future. This might be on paper as a drawing or using Lego to make a figure that shows how they feel.
- Blobs – clients take some adhesive putty or modelling putty and make a blob that demonstrates how they are feeling. This might be a sphere that they smash, or something stretched thin. It can be a very tactile way for clients to express themselves.
- Card sorts – card sorts of career management skills, such as the *Career Navigator* cards by Liane Hambly or the *What's Your Strength* cards by Katherine Jennick, are both useful ways of helping clients to understand themselves.
- Growth mindset – the belief that a person's capacities and talents can be improved over time. The power of 'YET'. Simply adding the word 'yet' to the statement 'I can't do that . . .' changes the individual's perception of themselves from static to fluid; unable to able.
- Reframing – a technique used to shift your mindset so you're able to look at a situation, person or relationship from a slightly different perspective. By challenging automatic negative thoughts, reframing opens up your mind to creative solutions, improving your ability to navigate and overcome challenges.

While writing this book, Chris ended up in hospital. He was waiting to see a doctor . . . as was a young person with ASC and ADHD (and their mum).

The young person wants to be a police officer. Following a careers conversation and talk through of things they could do, they confided they were worried about going onto a shared ward.

Reframe: Chris discussed how the people skills they would learn would help with joining the police later.

- Narrative – helping clients tell a story, or narrative, can provide context for their current situation and what might happen in the future. You can use all sorts of props for this.

Chris is a huge **Lego** fan.

As discussed in the Lego Guidance approach (published in the June 2017 edition of *Career Matters* magazine by the CDI), Lego remains a non-threatening medium for many clients to support career conversations.

If you are using Lego 'people', there is a diverse collection of pieces (representing different skin colours and disabilities – for example, you can get wheelchairs now) and different facial expressions. Recently, a young person made a figure to represent themselves which had a worried face. They couldn't say they were worried, but they could show it through the figure.

Include objects, or Lego pieces, to represent hobbies and interests like musical instruments, skateboards and spanners. If you don't have Lego, you can use other figures such as robots or animal toys.

Jules loves pipe cleaners and drawings!

Drawing is quite universal – you don't need to be particularly good at it to express your thoughts and feelings. Chris is good at drawing (as you can see from our illustrations); Jules . . . not so good. However, being less good than a client at something also offers an opportunity to redress the innate 'power' dynamic.

Pipe cleaners – cheap, easy to carry around, can be made into pretty much anything.

Have a look at 'social stories' and 'comic strip conversations' to see how these can be useful:

Social stories™ and comic strip conversations can help autistic people develop greater social understanding and help them stay safe.

The terms 'social story' and 'social stories' are trademarks originated and owned by Carol Gray.

They are short descriptions of a particular situation, event or activity, which include specific information about what to expect in that situation and why.

Social stories can be used to:

- develop independence, social skills and academic skills;
- help someone understand how others might behave or respond in a particular situation;
- help us understand the perspective of an autistic person and why they may respond or behave in a particular way;
- help cope with changes to routine and unexpected or upsetting events;
- provide positive feedback about areas of strength in order to develop self-esteem;
- model behaviour strategies (e.g. what to do when you are angry, how to cope with obsessions).

Social stories help:

- with sequencing (what comes next in a series of activities);
- with executive functioning (planning and organising);
- provide information about what might happen in a particular situation;
- give guidelines for behaviour;
- increase structure;
- reduce anxiety.

Creating or using a social story can help us understand how an autistic person perceives different situations.

To write a social story, you need to:

- picture the goal;
- gather information;
- tailor the text.

Stories should appeal to the interests of the person they are written for and avoid using words that may cause anxiety or distress.

The content and presentation of social stories should be appropriate to the person's age and level of understanding.

Use age-appropriate photographs, picture symbols or drawings with text to help people who have difficulty reading.

Have a title, introduction, body and conclusion.

Use gentle and supportive language.

Answer six questions: where, when, who, what, how and why?

For more information and guidelines on how to write social stories, see the resources section.

Comic strip conversations are simple visual representations of conversations.

They can show:

- the things that are actually said in a conversation;
- how people might feel;
- what people's intentions might be.

They use stick figures and symbols to represent social interactions and abstract aspects of conversation, and colour to represent the emotional content of a statement or message.

By seeing the different elements of a conversation presented visually, some of the more abstract aspects of social communication (such as recognising the feelings of others) are made more 'concrete' and are therefore easier to understand.

Comic strip conversations can help with understanding concepts.

People draw as they talk and use these drawings to learn.

Comic strip conversations can be used to plan for a situation in the future that may be causing anxiety or concern.

However, remember that plans can sometimes change. It's important to present the information in a way that allows for unexpected changes to a situation.

Some people may like to have their comic strip conversations in a notebook or saved on their smartphone or tablet so that they can refer to them as needed and easily recall key concepts.

Idea for your toolkit:

Having a range of different Lego faces or small objects that depict different mood states can be helpful. You could ask a client to pick faces or objects which represent themselves and where they are at. Using Lego, they can literally 'build' a picture. This can flag up any early concerns, especially where clients struggle to verbalise how they are feeling.

Opportunities

This could include discussing things like college, apprenticeships or higher education, but equally it could consider people in the client's network who can provide opportunities, or the opportunity, to try new things.

Activities that can promote exploration of opportunities:

- Posters and worksheets – many people are now giving consideration to making these inclusive, and there are lots of free resources and templates available. Do consider if you have too much information on display, though.
- Career Mapping – where clients 'map out' with help from the career practitioner what is possible, is another way clients can discover what is out there and how they relate to each other. There are lots of different ways this can be done, from mapping out on paper or a smart screen or making opportunity cards for clients to work with. This is a tactile way of working and can be repositioned and moved around.
- Career as a Journey – clients may reflect on the idea of a career as a journey. This perspective is particularly useful when clients feel 'stuck' or are fixated on understanding the paths to a particular job. The journey instead considers the career management skills they may need and the opportunities they may be able to take advantage of. Exploring a 'journey' that adds value and opens doors is a useful alternative to establishing a back-up plan.
- Cards sorts – using packs such as *Sunrise Career Guidance's Shape of Careers* or the *Panjango Top Trumps* can be helpful for clients to not only identify possible opportunities but also in their understanding of what is important to them.
- Software – using careers software, such as *Jed* or *EClips*, can be helpful in identifying opportunities. Do consider how people will be able to access the software independently.

Sector-specific and employer websites can be useful, but there are so many of them!

- Sometimes we are asked, 'How do you find these websites?'

  The answer is often word of mouth – work colleagues, attending CPD events or via the online careers community who share links online (such as via LinkedIn or Facebook). Increasingly, CPDs have less time to research and spend little time with colleagues due to pressures of delivery.
- The career websites of each home nation contain job profiles that include links to sector-specific websites and can be a useful place to start in finding these.
- Keeping up to date with careers information is important, so do put aside time to do some professional development and share with colleagues.
- Share with clients *how* to find information – or agree with them on who in their circle of support could help them do this. Simply giving people information is only a short-term solution.
- Careers Quizzes – can be fun and useful for self-discovery as well as opportunity awareness.
- Quizzes and assessments don't work for all students – they often lack subjective nuance and can be open to misinterpretation.
- Virtual work experience and tours are an easily accessible way for clients and their circles of support to explore and get a sense of a place prior to deciding on an actual visit or placement.
- Insight Videos – often shot by charities or sector bodies, offer an opportunity to take lived experience into account. Some good examples include:
  - ✔ videos by Kent & Medway Progression Federation aimed at students with additional needs who are considering university;
  - ✔ the award-winning short film *Listen,* in which nonspeaking autistic people talk about how nonspeakers are represented and provide guidance for changing the narrative.
- Podcasts – great for those of us with eyesight issues.
- Open Public Lectures, UCAS Subject Tasters and Massive Open Online Courses (MOOCs) – free online courses available for anyone to enrol.

Discuss *how* to find these in a careers session. They are a great way for people to find out what learning at a higher level feels like.

- Books – picture books can provide insight into what jobs look like . . . great for students who have more complex needs and don't get out in the world so much. Traditional career books and insight guides are good for better readers but may be off-putting for people who don't like lots of information.

- You may wish to work with your school or community librarian (if you have one) to build a library of not only career books but also 'reading around the subject' starter guides.
- Initial reading lists can be helpful to avoid overload – there is so much information on the internet that it can be hard to navigate.
- A prompt to clients to follow their own intellectual curiosity can lead to all sorts of new ideas.
- Work experience, work shadowing and volunteering – can be incredibly useful for providing insight.
  - ✔ We need to be mindful that it might not be straightforward for some people to 'just' arrange a visit or turn up at a workplace. They may need considerable support to make this step which, although seemingly straightforward to others, may be quite tricky.
  - ✔ Social stories can help.
  - ✔ Clients who access Adult Social Care still have the option to work. There is a legal duty under the Care Act 2014 to facilitate employment and volunteering opportunities for people with disabilities and other vulnerable adults.
- Supported Employment and Supported Internships – are personalised models for supporting disabled people to secure and retain paid employment, and businesses to employ valuable workers, using Vocational Profiling, job analysis and in-work support to learn the tasks required.
  - ✔ A vocational profile is a way of gathering information. It is a person-centred discovery document that is specifically related to work and supporting someone in finding a job. Go to the NDTi website for more information and some great templates.
- Self-employment and entrepreneurship are often overlooked but can be the easiest way for some disabled people to configure their working lives to suit them.
  - ✔ *You've Got This!* Offered by the SAMEE Project supports individuals through the development of skills needed to explore self-employment as a viable career option. It is created to cater to the needs of learners with learning support needs.
  - ✔ *Independent and Work Ready* offers virtual training and work experience in product design leading to a qualification. Participants design products including key rings, T-shirts caps, tote bags, which they print and sell. The service is disability-led and run.

- When inviting employers to give a talk or attend a careers event, ask them to bring practical props/items or an activity. Providing the employer with a pen profile of the students' needs can also be helpful.
- Circles of support – can help students explore who they have in their own network, who they could talk to and who can support them with different aspects of opportunity awareness and decision-making. There is more information on Circles of support in Chapter 8.

Idea for your toolkit:

Careers adviser, Lis McGuire, RCDP (Sunrise Careers – or follow her on LinkedIn), uses magnetic figures that connect together to help clients explore who they have in their own networks and within their circle of support's networks. A great tactile resource that visibly shows 'connections'.

Decisions

Much of this book (and others for career professionals, such as *Creative Coaching: Theory Into Practice*) considers strategies to support decision-making.

Historically, within Careers practice there was a focus on helping clients to make decisions in a single careers session, often weighing up choice A and choice B, using just pros and cons.

Decision-making is often far more subtle and complex. For some students, the above somewhat one-dimensional approach might work. Yet, for many, they need time to process their ideas and reflect.

Our role can help clients consider a wider viewpoint on decision-making, helping them determine how they wish to decide, how much time they need and what they need to do to make a decision; it is not exclusively about helping them make a choice in a single session!

Some students will require several sessions to work through their ideas. Some may need to see us and then go and do some research or undertake some experiential learning. Others will find their career guidance session a catalyst for change, which kicks off a greater exploration of their hopes and dreams.

Many people will make a decision to do X or Y in the future – when we catch up with them at a later date, their ideas are totally different. The guidance session started them thinking far more deeply about what they wanted to do, becoming a 'kick start' to think differently.

- When a decision is made in a session, it is often beneficial for clients to consider how much time they may need to reflect on their choice to ensure it is the right one for them.

Example – a student who made a decision to do an apprenticeship in a careers session. We planned through their next steps . . . what they would do to find an apprenticeship and the steps to help with their transition.

The student came back about a month later and said they were now on another path. As we unpicked things, they said the reality of actually planning to do an apprenticeship helped them realise that it wasn't what they really wanted to do; it was a fantasy.

This idea of a 'fantasy stage' aligns with Ginzberg's developmental theory; the guidance process made the career real to the student and then, on reflection, helped them to realise that their initial choice (and plan of action) was the wrong one.

- Some people may need to research the choices they *don't* want to pursue, to double-check that it isn't for them. It is easier to overlook things we assume we won't like.
- People may struggle to make choices while escalated, tired, overwhelmed, unwell and/or hungry.

You can use a decision-making profile to establish:

- How people like to get information.
- How they want choices presented.
- How can we help with understanding?
- When the best and worst times are for them to make decisions.

- We should be mindful of our own physical and emotional state; we may struggle to support others if we are not operating at our best.
- Decisions can't be forced. Returning to Rogerian conditions of empathy, congruence and unconditional positive regard is a useful reminder of what we are doing and why.
- Does the client need a movement break?
- Are they overwhelmed?
- Do they need time to process a question or what has been explored so far? Have a look at the section on Questions in Chapter 2. Give your clients, and yourself, TIME and SPACE.

Transitions

The importance of successful transitions is often overlooked in Career Planning. It is much more prominent in the world of 'Preparing for Adulthood' and 'Transition Support':

- Help clients consider what help they might require with their plans and from whom.
- Transition is not 'done to' or 'done for' clients but 'done with'. We know from our professional training that co-construction of plans is far more effective and meaningful than being dictated to.

Some of the barriers to successful transitions are worth considering and reflecting on:

- Is the client tired? Do they need a rest before planning their transition activities, and/or does it need to take place in another session?
- Do they have sufficient skills to plan without their circle of support?
- What is the process that links the career session and action planning into the wider transition process?
- How much is too much? Your client may only need two to three actions as part of their next steps. They may need 'just one thing'! What is the right amount at this stage for them?
- Will you be able to see them again? If not, is there a way to 'hand over' support for transitional activities or follow-up to someone else? Does the client *choose* for them to be in their circle of support?

'Important to'

We can use different ways of capturing what is 'important to' our clients.

The NDTi has some free templates in their *Preparing for Adulthood* toolkit.

Or you can make your own whiteboard cards.

These are playing card-sized whiteboards (available from online retailers) to capture ideas and thoughts about the future.

As the client is talking, capture key nuggets of information that are important to them. These can include:

- values;
- pathways of interest such as apprenticeships or education;
- key people in their support network;

- ideas such as starting a business or travel;
- possible jobs;
- how they might like to live in the future.

Write these 'nuggets' on the individual boards and place them down between the client and yourself. You can also draw pictures if this is more suitable for your client, or use symbols instead.

Use a coloured pen that works for them (whether due to their additional needs or just psychological preferences) while remaining inclusive.

As the session flows, depending on what is agreed upon in terms of purpose, you can use some of the cards as jumping-off points for discussion.

They can identify:

- where we have questions;
- what we might do (or not do) about them;
- areas for further research;
- people who can help them.

We sometimes get involved with career or route mapping, where we explore possible pathways to their career goals. With this, on each whiteboard, one of us can write each option or step on the career journey as we identify it via discussion and/or research – often ending up with multiple paths and choices.

The hands-on nature of these cards, and the ability to reposition them, take them away, wipe off the words or question marks or just flip them over, makes the approach work for the students.

It is this kinaesthetic nature which many people tap into.

It gives clients ownership to leave ideas in play or take them away as they work through what is possible for them.

Clients who don't like the idea of 'taking options away' (off the table) may prefer the cards being flipped over, representing ideas they could return to if they wish.

Supporting families

- Many parents and carers have not been given the tools and information they need to effectively support person-centred planning for their young people.

- Some parents and carers may have additional needs themselves.
- The complexity of the educational and training system is a challenge.
- Ask if they require advocacy or support themselves.

Understanding where and how you can tap into greater support for parents and carers, as well as your immediate client, is important as one affects the other. This might be via specialist local authority services, social services, charities or via an education provider.

- Consider running sessions exclusively for parents and carers. Explain CEIAG, Mental Capacity and Transition Planning. Give them some Person-Centred Planning tools and resources to work with their young people.
- There are resources specifically aimed at families who are supporting another family member to plan and make choices. Add them to your toolkit (links are in the resources section).
- There is a great resource specifically aimed at young people with limited life expectancy.

Short Lives – Parallel planning

- These are great resources specifically aimed at young people with limited life expectancy.
- Together for short lives have resources for young people, families and professionals.

'Every young person, from the age of 14, should be supported to be at the centre of preparing for approaching adulthood and for the move to adult services. Their families should be supported to prepare for their changing role.'[1]

Just one thing

If a client finds **just one thing** impactful in their career planning journey, we have made a difference. They may have a very different perspective on 'positive outcomes' from our own or the organisations we work for.

Sam has cerebral palsy.

Cerebral palsy is the name for a group of lifelong conditions that affect movement and co-ordination. It's caused by a problem with the brain that develops before, during or soon after birth.

This impacts their lives in a number of ways, including:

- an unsteady gait when walking;
- some difficulty in expressing language due to differences in their facial muscles;
- fatigue when carrying out physical tasks (such as moving around large buildings, using stairs, writing for extended periods, etc.).

Sam's mum asked Jules to see them as they had failed to engage with the school careers adviser, and Mum was concerned they would miss out on potential future options.

Jules checked with Sam to see if they wanted help with career planning.

The contract with Sam and Mum was clear that Sam would decide which information was shared with Mum and/or the school.

Sam and Jules discussed their:

- current educational attainment and challenges;
- hopes and aspirations for the future;
- anxieties about mobility;
- anxieties about being understood when speaking (particularly on the telephone – Sam had a range of superb strategies to avoid ever talking on the phone);
- circle of support and how this could best be used to Sam's advantage;
- views on disability;

A plan was established, which included:

- a challenge for Sam to accept the opinions of his teachers about his academic ability;
- a range of research about both the University and alternatives;
- identified people to support and encourage the actions agreed upon;
- information on learning to drive as a disabled young person;
- an offer of a place on a disability-focused project we happened to be running;
- the opportunity to practice using the telephone with 'safe' people.

Outcomes

- University applied for – places offered.
- Driving lessons taken – test passed – car purchased using the Motability scheme.
- After only two 'phone practices' . . . UCAS contacted by phone during clearing to secure a better course than those originally applied for.
- A fantastic publication for other disabled young people (from the disability project group).
- Sam and Mum are both happy.

Three years later, Jules received an email from Sam.

> I don't know if you remember me, but I wanted to tell you that you changed my life. I'm on my industry placement year for my degree, working in a hospital, and I've just phoned through to a ward to secure a bed for someone. I could never have done that if you hadn't got me to use the telephone.

Just that one thing – which Jules hardly registered at the time because for her it was such an easy and quick practical offer – changed their life.

Hopefully, the rest of the guidance also had some impact; however, from Sam's perspective, the phone skills were the invaluable part.

It is also worth noting that for clients who struggle to make choices, or to plan, giving them 'just one thing' as a suggestion to try may be do-able. Once they find they are able to do one thing, they are more likely to choose to do more.

Ren has PDA

'Demand avoidance' involves not being able to do certain things at certain times, either for yourself or others, and also refers to the things we do in order to avoid demands.

It's a **natural human trait** – avoiding demands is something we all do to different degrees and for different reasons.

When demand avoidance is more significant, there can be many possible reasons for this – it could be situational; related to physical or mental health; or related to a developmental or personality condition.

PDA (Pathological Demand Avoidance) is widely understood to be a profile on the autism spectrum, involving the avoidance of everyday demands and the use of 'social' strategies as part of this avoidance.

Ren said Jules would not be able to help them as they would not do anything Jules asked them to!

They then went on to describe numerous examples of how this manifested with family, peers and teachers.

Jules asked if she could suggest 'just one thing' with the understanding that there was no expectation that anything would result from it. Agreement was given with a cheery smile and a 'You know I won't do it, right?' response.

She suggested Carol Dweck's TED talk about Growth Mindset might be an interesting watch.

Several months later Ren ran up to Jules in a corridor and said, 'I just wanted you to know . . . you started a snowball! How did you get me to watch that video?' And before I could reply . . . 'Oh, you didn't did you!?'

They then went on to describe some of the positive feelings they were now experiencing from being proactive, acts of kindness and reframing their fear of failure into a view that they just couldn't do something 'yet'. Ren booked another careers appointment shortly afterwards.

Helping students explore a mixture of different viewpoints can be helpful, as well as learning how to distinguish and use different information within career planning. For example, videos shot and posted by an institution and separately by the students can help provide a nuanced balance and contrast well with each other.

Mix-and-match – you can combine different approaches and sensory tools to help them show what they are good at, what skills and interests they have or which areas of career management they wish to develop.

It is easy to make assumptions about what clients will, or won't, take from the guidance interventions they experience with us. Feedback on what worked – or didn't – helps us to reflect on how we can develop our practice. Try out different tools and strategies to see what works for you and your clients.

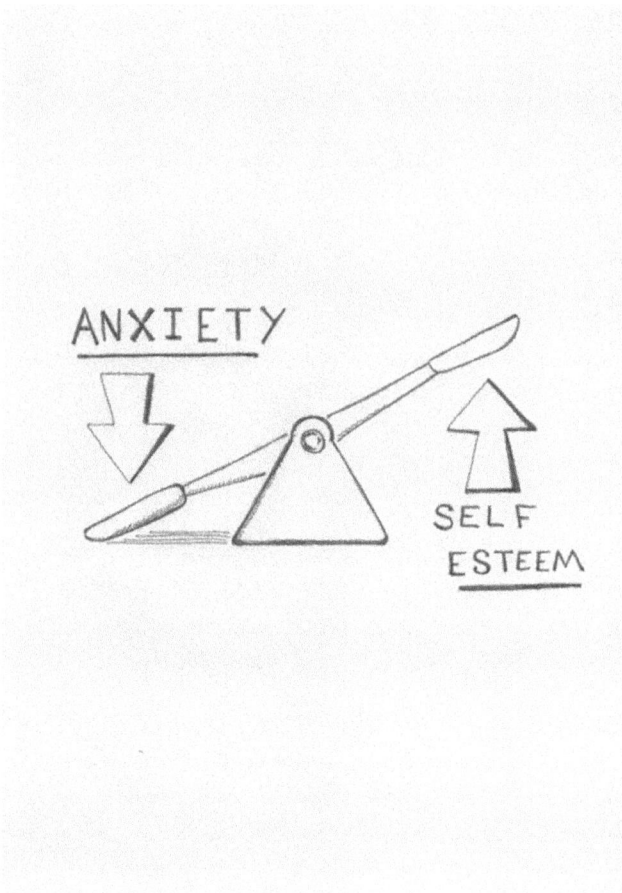

The resources section has links to lots of further information and tools to add to your toolkit. You can access it via the QR code and URL at the start of the book.

For some explanations about different impairments, and some of the words and phrases used within learning support and disability communities, have a look at our glossary.

Note

1 https://www.togetherforshortlives.org.uk/get-support/information-about-your-childs-care/transition-to-adult-care/moving-to-adult-services-what-to-expect/

Chapter 8
How we organise interactions

Length of session

The Career Development Institute recommends that at least 45 minutes be allowed for every guidance interview to allow time for exploration and self-discovery. This is also reflected in the UK governments' guidance on Career Guidance and Personal Guidance 1:1 interviews.

Being client centred takes priority over too ridged compliance with this recommendation; considering what our clients need must come first.

For some clients – with ADHD or Chronic Fatigue, for example – 45 minutes may be too long for them to sit or to maintain concentration.

To build in this flexibility is important for successful career sessions. So how can this be done?

Introducing . . .

Start with an introduction of who you are and what you do. The opportunity to talk to small groups prior to seeing people individually is ideal. Also, consider doing a written 'explainer' and/or a video.

Examples of things to explain . . .

OUR JOB ROLE

is to help people to:

- think about future options;
- make their own plans and choices;
- check that they are aware of all their options;
- make suggestions about things that might help.

It is NOT to:

- tell people what to do.

SUPPORT

- We don't expect people to do everything on their own.
- We can help people find any support they may need.

RESPECT

Everybody is . . .

- different;
- important;
- valued.

IMPARTIALITY

- This means we don't have our own agenda about other people's plans.
- It's all about you!

Explain how the sessions are client-led.

QUESTIONS

- There are no right or wrong answers. It is not a test.
- We ask questions to find out what is important to you.
- You can ask us questions too.

CONFIDENTIALITY

We will keep your information private unless:

- you ask us to share it (e.g. with a tutor, job coach or parent);

or

- there is a concern about keeping people safe.

ACCESS

- This is how to book an appointment . . . this is where we will be on Tuesday lunchtimes . . . this is how to get in touch with us. . .
- If it's difficult for you to get to us, or meet us, please let us know – we can arrange to meet online, in another place or with another person.

- We really want you to be comfortable – please let us know if you need anything to help you. Bring a fidget toy or doodle pad if you would like.

You could also use video or photos to show a building, how to get there and how to get in or to show clients any other members of the team they might meet.

- For clients with high levels of anxiety a good introduction means they know what to expect, so they can then focus on their ideas rather than worry about meeting us.
- Talking to students in class means that staff hear the same introduction as students, making them aware of what we do.

Fixed but flexible

In a setting where the sessions are fixed:

- Have an agreement with the setting to lengthen or shorten the sessions if needed.
- Have the option to 'walk and talk' – where clients who need to move can have their career session while walking around a communal area or outdoor space. This can be useful for clients who:
  - ✔ struggle in the formal setting of a room;
  - ✔ feel less anxious in an outdoor space;
  - ✔ require movement to regulate.
- Offer options to help with regulation and focus, such as:
  - ✔ fidget toys;
  - ✔ a choice of seating options;
  - ✔ pens/pencils and paper.

Drop-Ins

Drop-Ins can take lots of different forms and can be run in a wide range of different settings – consideration does need to be given to your own wellbeing so ensure you get a break!

They allow people to access careers guidance on their terms, outside the formal parameters of 'booked appointments'.

They can be incredibly empowering if handled with the care of a standard (booked) careers session.

Chris was working with a client who was too anxious to come to their 'booked' career appointment.

Several attempts had been made to see them, including attending with support from their Teaching Assistant as well as their favourite tutor. They still couldn't cope with attending.

In the school, we advertised our offer to students on the school website, social media platforms and newsletter which went to students, teachers, parents and carers. This included our lunchtime drop-in.

The drop-in was for 20 minutes at the start of the lunch period, with the rest of the time available for Chris to eat and take a break.

Our student showed up one day 'out of curiosity' to see what it was like; they asked what Chris did and why, before leaving after 10 minutes.

The next week (when Chris was back in school) they rocked up again, offering up that they had 'no idea what they were going to do after Year 11' and, after a gentle initial chat, left again.

The next week . . . who should turn up but our student! 'There is no way I am going to college! You can't make me apply or do anything!'

Chris confirmed that he would never tell them what to do but was happy to discuss ideas and listen to them. Again, off they went after 15 minutes.

You can guess what happened next.

Following week, they popped by again with a smile.

. . . and so it continued for about a term and a half. They would pop by each week, continue to explore their ideas and talk about their thoughts since the previous week.

By the end of this, they had applied to college for a course they loved the idea of.

Next drop-in topic – interview preparation: to shake hands or not? Look just above and between the eyes if struggling to make eye contact.

End of term, they popped by with a huge grin on their face . . . 'I'm going to college! I was accepted after the interview.'

Offering lunchtime drop-ins helped to create an inclusive service which is client centred. #careersimpact

Flexed appointments

A flexible model is where the length of the session is dictated by the client.

Crucially, clients remain in control of the length of time each session is, the format of action plans and to a certain extent, location of the session.

A system should be agreed upon in advance with the education provider and a 'running order' agreed for each day so that staff and students are aware of who will be next.

Jules also uses this model to give students the opportunity to explain to their peers what to expect. Each student returns to class following their interview, collects the next student and walks with them to their interview.

The students are usually brilliant at explaining our role, and they say really useful things to each other like, 'It's OK, you can just be yourself', and 'you should go and talk to her; she has a big brain'.

Thirty-minute fixed session (with repeats)

In several settings, we offer 30-minute sessions, where students will have more than one session based on their needs.

The initial 30-minute session is to see where they are at and how things are going, as well as to help the client understand what is possible within the remit of a careers guidance session and how the client and adviser will work together.

It can also be used to build a focus for following sessions.

The following session or sessions (depending on need) are then used to provide the intervention, focused on their needs.

For some clients, the 30-minute session can be enough to resolve their concerns, but from experience, this is a rarity.

A good example of where this format has worked well is with the following client:

A student who was unsure of what they wanted to try out:

They were anxious and had been putting themselves under pressure. Stress levels were high.

We had agreed in advance to work together for just 30 minutes to reduce their anxiety.

To help them identify what they wanted to explore, we agreed to try a card sort (using job cards with names of different occupations on). In this instance, the *Panjango Top Trumps* cards.

Within this, we agreed that we wouldn't make any judgement about what 'came up'; we would just identify possibilities (to revisit in our next 30-minute session).

Chris asked the client to sort their cards into three piles, representing what they 'definitely didn't like', 'what interested them', and 'maybes' represented by three cards of my own making:

Once they had done this, Chris asked them to sort the 'Yes' pile into patterns (importantly based on their ideas and concepts, not Chris').

Chris then asked them to see if any of the 'maybe?' cards should be added.

This led to a discussion about what was meaningful to them as patterns of possibility, followed by a summary of the session – including photos of the cards, and an agreement to revisit these possibilities in the next session.

Session 2

- revisited the photographs taken during the card sort;
- explored what to do next;
- agreed to identify the top three 'options/jobs' which interested them and which they would then like to 'try out'.

Three appealed to them: hairdressing, retail and comic book illustration.

Then how they would like to explore these areas and 'try them out'.

Some of the previous work done in the 'career introductions' had explored that many of us won't know what we wish to do until we are closer to 25.

They decided they wished to work with the work experience co-ordinator at the college to find supported work experience in hairdressing and search for a part-time job in retail.

In addition, they would work with the Art teacher in the college to explore making their own comics.

This provided them with a way forward, which wouldn't have been possible without taking the pressure off by splitting the session into two halves.

Room set-up

Room set-up, whether virtual or physical, is easy to overlook and not something we always have control of.

- Arrive early to set up and get things in order.

Consider your safety and that of your clients:

- being able to access the space easily without something between you and the door (whether a table or the client) is important, as well as having a way to call for help (whether a panic button, walkie-talkie or phone);
- being in a room where there is monitoring glass is another safety feature that is worth considering.

Beyond this, be mindful of:

- strong smells (from flowers, your own perfume or aftershave, cleaning products or even students who have previously used the room . . . can we say teenage sweat!);
- bright or flickering lights;
- not setting up a power dynamic with your seat being higher than theirs (or vice versa), and if you can . . . offer a choice of different chairs (sofas or beanbags);
- offering a set-up where you can sit side by side (so they don't have to make eye contact);
- asking if there is anything they would like to change about the room to make them feel more comfortable;
- preparing any resources or props, so they are easily at hand and you don't have to go searching for them.

Chris: With my own ADHD I also set my resources out in a set manner each time so, I don't mislay them or forget where they are (as my brain is prone to do!). I also have out a fiddle toy (for clients who have ADHD and/ or anxious) and invite them to use if they wish. Often I have one as well, which can be useful for mirroring and putting them at ease.

Jules: I set out a selection of fiddle toys, coloured paper and pens/pencils + a card sort and a couple of other items on a table next to the main seating and tell people to feel free to pick up anything they want while we're talking.

Having access to other environments (alternatives to a traditional 'careers' room) can change the possibility of what can occur during an interaction:

- Can you offer 'walk and talk' sessions?
- Do you have access to a sensory room?
- Can you use a break-out space? For example, there may be a common room with a pool table and comfortable sofas, or an outside sitting area. For some clients, these are the spaces where they feel more comfortable. Being mindful of how clients feel in different spaces and being aware of how they react to different spaces is a really useful reflection for our work.
- If looking to use outside or community spaces as part of your work, make sure you have permission from the setting you find yourself in, have a suitable risk assessment completed and consider confidentiality.

In virtual environments:

- arrive early and check if the software and internet connection are working;
- check the height of the camera and how you appear on the screen – the last thing anyone needs is a shot up your nose! It's useful to get a decent amount of your body as well as your face to make you look more like a person than a floating head;
- check what is behind you, blur your background or add a peaceful virtual background – if your dirty washing is in view, or your background is very 'busy', this can be distracting;
- be mindful of background noises and the wider environment, such as traffic noises, which can be distracting for both yourself and clients;
- if possible, try and book yourself into a space that will have minimal disruption and distractions;
- check with the client whether they are okay with using the software you are planning to use for the virtual or video call, or whether they prefer an alternative format (if available);
- provide them with an emergency contact (either phone and/or email) in case there are problems with the connection
- In the future, will we be meeting in Virtual Reality environments?
- What considerations would we make then?

Through such tools, perhaps our sessions could become more inclusive and accessible.

Consider a future where we might meet with clients via robotic intermediaries.

Food for thought: In Japan, there is the Dawn Avatar Café in Nihonbashi run by people who have physical impairments, some of whom are unable to leave their beds and only have minimal movement of eyes and mouths. Through computers and software, they operate remote robots at the café, through which they serve and interact with the customers.

- What are our perceptions and potential biases regarding what we consider disabled people are capable of doing?

Someone else in the room?

- Will there be a member of the teaching staff in the session?
- Are parents/carers invited?
- Will there be a Communication Support Worker (CSW) or Interpreter present?

Include them in your contract at the beginning of your intervention and send them the same pre-session information as the client.

Establish clearly that:

- you would like them to help with communication between you and the client, but NOT to talk for them;
- they should not offer their own opinion unless requested to by the client – leave time at the end for any questions or comments;
- they are bound by the same confidentiality agreement as you and the client.

A core part of developing a positive working relationship is ensuring that there is a clear understanding of each other's roles and boundaries. A discussion over a cup of tea or coffee when setting up the delivery (before any sessions or delivery starts) is a useful way to iron out what the working relationship will look like (which often varies from setting to setting).

Pros and cons:

There are some scenarios where having a staff member or parent present works really well and there are some which create a problematic environment for practise and client-centred work.

You may find that it comes down to your own skills in managing group dynamics to hold space for the client's voice, so it doesn't get swamped by others.

It might also depend on your relationship with the staff member or parent and whether there is mutual respect.

Some of the risks:

- the client might feel unable to express their own ideas or thoughts, without the judgement or domination (explicit or implicit; perceived or actual) of the other person.

Even those with whom they have a seemingly positive working relationship can sometimes be unintentionally oppressive or constraining. People may not want to disappoint their teacher or parent and go along with a choice for their sake rather than their own.

- parents or carers may seek to exercise their will and push what they feel is right for the client. This is usually well intentioned but can sometimes result in the client hiding their true thoughts or feelings about a given situation or set of choices.

We can reflect that it is for good reason that career development professionals seek to create a safe, confidential and non-judgemental working environment that attends to the core conditions (as per Carl Rogers), enabling the clients' voices to be heard.

Some of the advantages:

- having a trusted person in attendance can be a positive experience, which can be incredibly enabling.

Some people need a support worker who is familiar with their communication, and some feel less anxious with another person in the room.

Theoretically, this idea taps into Community Interaction Theory by Bill Law as well as the Systems Theory Framework of Career Development by Wendy Patton & Mary McMahon which, each in their own way, reflect upon how career ideas are developed within a wider social context.

- Remember that having someone else present is the client's choice if they have the mental capacity to make this decision.

Circles of support

Not everyone can, or chooses to, make decisions independently.

A circle of support is a group of people that a person chooses to support in making their own decisions about their life.

Circles were developed to support individuals in becoming connected in the community and in making friendships and relationships.

For most of us, we form these naturally – when we are troubled, we call on our family and friends to share our pain or joy and to help us think through what we can do. For people who are disempowered, like some people with learning disabilities, this does not happen.

As individuals, and as families, they may become isolated and have very few people around them. It is in these circumstances that circles of friends/support need to be developed.

Circles are a group of people who meet to help somebody achieve what they would like to do in their life. It might be, for example, about expanding their social circle, finding somewhere to live or participating in a leisure or work activity. The client decides whom they want to invite, what they talk about and where the circle should meet.

- Helping our clients to develop a Circle will offer them ongoing support with planning and decision-making. Inevitably, they move on from our help and support, so giving their Circle the tools to help them on their career journey is an effective method of transition support.
- Check if your clients have an existing circle, and who is in it.

Case Studies: Working with learning support staff
Setting 1: A boarding school in England

Students with additional needs are prioritised for Careers Interviews at the start of Year 11 (building on the wider and previous support in place).

The SENCO attends the initial intervention and provides us with a pen profile of the student's needs as well as the wider social context (this particular school has students from lots of different countries).

The SENCO lets the CDP lead and contributes pertinent questions and points to help with exploring possibilities.

They are in affect a 'coach' complementing the CDP's 'guidance'-led questions.

This works really well.

Of note, the culture of the school is very reserved, and one where visitors to the school are treated with the utmost respect by students. It requires hard work to create an environment of trust and to put students at ease.

For some students, this can be a challenge – due to learnt behaviour, they don't wish to offend.

Having the additional coaching skills from the SENCO alongside the CDP guidance, as an additional trusted adult in this 'triumvirate' approach, is incredibly helpful. Their reassurance aids in opening up and unlocking the students' wishes.

This SENCO also subscribes to the CDI code of ethics, which we agree upon at the start of each session.

When explaining boundaries around confidentiality and agenda, the SENCO confirms that they are also covered and won't go back to other teachers at the school with what the student tells us (e.g. if they say that they don't like a particular subject or teacher).

Setting 2: A group in England that provides support for young people who have a wide range of needs and abilities.

Three career development professionals provide Careers Guidance across the group of schools and a college, working with the SENCO to offer a targeted approach to help support those students most in need.

For many of these students, there are either additional issues at home, or they don't 'fit' the available options in the local offer due to the complexity of their situations.

This can be due to compound issues such as not being able to travel easily between towns, living in the countryside with no access to transport or being unable to fund transport costs (even with Local Authority support); being too anxious to venture out or caught up in situations where they won't go to a town, due to other people there that they don't get on with, or having had confrontations with the police or similar.

The SENCO brings a nuanced understanding of what each young person is capable of and their barriers, which can be incredibly insightful and useful and, in many cases, difficult to ascertain via a pen profile or information provided in advance.

In some instances, young people will over or underestimate their abilities, which won't be reflected in predicted grades and, in many cases, will vary by context.

It is this considered level of insight, which we both respectively bring, that works alongside mutual appreciation and respect for each other's professions.

It differs from the coaching approach used by the SENCO in the previous setting – it is far more solution-focused and set within each given context, where there seem to be very few options for some of the young people we are focused on helping.

There are often very specific issues at play which are carefully addressed and discussed with the young person who is just as key to finding or identifying possible solutions as the SENCO or CDP. This is more akin to a team-around-the-child or Circle of Support approach.

The SENCO respects the CDI ethics we work under and works to provide the safe place students need to engage and plan.

- Tell your SENCOs – the Careers Enterprise Company now offers a SENCO Development Course: 'Understanding Pathways and Career Opportunities'. Follow the link in our resources section.

What do you do when you have an overbearing parent/carer or member of the teaching staff in the room? How can these situations be handled so the young person's voice isn't left swamped or absent?

Case Study:

Working with a young person we'll call Trey, who needed extra time to process information and had a physical disability - their fine motor co-ordination was tricky (but not impossible). They had low academic attainment and were on a reduced timetable.

Careers meeting with Trey and their parents:

Welcoming them into the room, the CDP introduced themselves and explained who they worked for. Immediately, one of the parents declared, 'I need to tell you where we are at . . .' followed by a list of their needs and worries.

CDP listened, recognised their worries and explained how the session would work.

I am going to focus all my attention on Trey, this isn't that I'm being rude but, they are the most important person in the room so it's important we hear from them. If you have any questions, please do feel free to ask at the end but I want to give Trey as much time and space as possible to answer and think about things. Is that ok?

Within this session, the Mum tried to answer a couple of questions for Trey (without giving them time to answer), but because contracting had been agreed upon at the start the CDP was able to (politely) come back to what we agreed and say to them, 'Do you remember how we were going to give Trey time to answer? Let's give them a bit longer.'

This session continued, and after some exploration, it became apparent that Trey was interested in catering and becoming a chef.

One of the parents said, 'Well, this isn't going to be possible with their needs!'

CDP response: There were some options around this which could be possible and researched if they wished.

CDP explained the principle of reasonable adjustments, as well as the specialist courses at the local college. In addition to this, they discussed Supported Employment, adjusted or inclusive apprenticeships and provided Trey and their family with some links and references.

Once addressed, we then turned the session towards looking at solutions, exploring who would do what and by when. Trey having an equal say explained how he would like a one-to-one visit to look around the local college to see what the place was like.

Through links with the local college, via the school SENCO, this was set up.

By the end of the session, the parents had moved from sceptical to embracing the possibilities alongside Trey.

This was through:

- careful exploration of options;
- agreeing on an approach at the start;
- placing Trey at the centre.

It also utilised knowledge of Transactional Analysis. The CDP maintained being in an Adult state, which pulled the parents into the same state (out of Critical/Controlling Parent).

- Are pen profiles provided before seeing clients? Are these provided on the day or beforehand?
- What do you need on the pen profiles for them to be effective?
- What pre-session information can you send to clients?

Pen Profiles (which may be called Pen Passports, Student Overviews or something similar) are incredibly useful when people have additional needs and/or complex pastoral needs. Being given an overview can help provide context and insight, not just into what their needs are but how they manifest for that particular individual.

> *When you meet one person with Autism, you've met one person with Autism.*
> —Dr Stephen Shore

A poor example of a pen profile would be simply a list of student names and conditions.

For example,
CT – ADHD/Anxiety
BT – ADHD/ASC
HL – ASC
JT – ADHD/ASC/Anxiety

It doesn't tell you anything constructive and just reinforces the medical model of disability, defining each student by their condition, rather than contextualising it within their lives.

In contrast, what makes a good pen profile?

- a student passport, where students create their own pen profile which they are happy to share with teachers and visitors.

It includes not only a list of their needs but also things they like (including hobbies and subjects), how they like to learn, triggers and strategies for coping with difficult times.

- Ask your schools if they can provide such a profile. Talk to them about what you found useful on it.

Things we have found useful include:

- Communication preferences;
- Preferred Name;
- Pronouns;
- Condition(s);
- How these manifest in different contexts for this individual;

- Things that provoke anxiety or overwhelming feelings;
- Preferred Learning / Coping Strategies;
- Predicted Grades, Key Support.

A profile might look something like this:

Preferred Name: Matilda
Pronouns: they/them
Communication: mostly uses speech. When anxious, may find speaking difficult and switch to using an iPad or whiteboard. If communication stops, take a break
Conditions(s): ASC, Anxiety

How these manifest in different contexts:

School is challenging, with groups of more than five often becoming quiet and unresponsive. Prone to outbursts when stressed. Dislikes eye contact.

Preferred Learning / Coping Strategies:

Has an exit card to use when needs to take air. Will take themselves to a quiet space in the Additional Education Needs (AEN) room to find balance, especially if overwhelmed. Struggles to handle praise, but this is improving. Uses visual diagrams to process ideas and likes the colour blue when creating these. Dislikes loud noises or people talking too quickly.

Predicted Grades:

GCSEs English: 4 Maths: 4 Science (combined): 5 Art: 3 DT: 4 MFL: 4 History: 6 ICT: 4

Key Support:

Ms. Bobbins (TA) is a key support in the Additional Education Needs room. SENCO is a key link with parents.

Mr. Smith is Youth Group leader and supports the exploration of career ideas outside of school.

Relevant Additional Information:

Attends community youth group outside of school, where they have been thriving and have started to learn street dance. They have developed a wider group of friends and extended their peer network, but days in school following the youth group they can be slightly 'burnt out' and may require more time in the AEN room to find balance.

- How does your Careers Guidance link with transition and pastoral arrangements in the setting?

The resources section has links to lots of further information and tools to add to your toolkit. You can access it via the QR code and URL at the start of the book.

For some explanations about different impairments and some of the words and phrases used within learning support and disability communities, have a look at our glossary.

Chapter 9
Action planning and information sharing

Action planning

- The action plan is a summative document and should not drive the process.
- The client should have ownership of both content and format.
- The structure of the action plan should be as simple as possible to allow for flexibility.
- A variety of formats should be available (written, verbal, pictoral, etc.).

It is really important before starting delivery to have a candid discussion to explore how the careers guidance which is being delivered links with the transition support and arrangements within school and college as well as the Local Authority and parents/carers.

This can affect everything from the format of action plans to the extent to which you can be creative in your approach and how the client's voice is captured.

- In whose interests are the action plans and sessions?
- Have the discussion with your settings before any delivery.
- Show examples of action plans.
- Agree on a clear strategy about who is responsible for any follow-up and/or support work.

Historically, career development professionals would provide independent Careers Guidance and attend Annual and Transitional Reviews.

In recent years, due to budget cuts in England, this has become less frequent as schools and colleges prioritise their resources. This means in many cases, career development professionals will deliver their Careers Guidance intervention and then the information from the session will be sent to the SENCO and used to inform the reviews.

Scotland, Wales and Northern Ireland use a centralised approach to Careers Guidance and Transition support which allows for more engagement with Learning Support systems.

Unless a clear information flow (both ways) is established there is a risk of creating a problematic situation where the careers work sits in isolation and doesn't feed into the wider transition processes.

There is also a risk that information isn't shared with parents/carers and others in a circle of support.

- Negotiate time with Learning Support staff to discuss outcomes and the ability to set up follow-up sessions with clients as needed.
- Set up referral processes where the career development professional can refer to supporting keyworkers for follow-up work, and Learning Support staff can also refer clients for more careers support.

Time to help other professionals understand our roles and processes are key to avoiding misunderstanding.

This includes the oft misinterpreted idea that Careers Guidance is a 'magic bullet' whereby we will come up with the options for our clients in each session, who will then choose their favourite (in the session), and then voila . . . have their choice made. Rather than it being part of a multifaceted process of reflection, discovery and research; which attends to the emerging understanding and needs of each client, where more than one session may be (in many cases) required to support our clients. Especially if they need to go away, consider and attend open days, speak to parents/carers and continue their research (outside of the confines of the session).

Things to consider when you're writing a plan:

- What will make young people feel good when they have taken that first step?
- Be alongside the young person and undertake a task with them (rather than FOR them).
- The process should be tailored to the young person's way of thinking.
- Success should be defined by the young person.
- Goals can be long or short term.
- People can take action without having a specific goal in mind.
- Some may find goal setting and SMART action planning a challenge.

SMART/Er

Specific, **M**easurable, **A**greed/Attainable, **R**ealistic, **T**ime-bound/**E**nergising and/or engaging

Do we need all the letters in SMART to make a plan?

- Setting tight timescales can be particularly anxiety provoking for some clients – a rough idea of time might be useful, but you can attach the **T** (**T**ime) to yourself rather than the plan ('I'll check in with you next month to see how you're getting on').
- The **M** – measurable can be mis-used to measure 'success'. For the client, success may be emotional – feeling better, more confident, more valued by others. It may be being able to catch a bus on their own, make a phone-call. If we **M**easure success based on outcomes from other people's agendas we risk losing the meaning for clients.
- **S**pecific goals may be something to address later – when the client has had some practice trying things, generating ideas and so on . . . It may be more appropriate to outline broader goals 'to make a decision that's right for me', and recontract at a later stage.
- **R**ealistic – be aware of Ableism. How often do we hear people saying that a career idea is 'unrealistic' for a disabled person? Does it matter what career ideas we have as long as we develop the skills to make choices, reframe, retry, rethink . . .

Some people do not have any concept of a future self and may find goal setting anxiety provoking and/or overwhelming.

Those who are unaccustomed to making plans may be compliant with other people suggesting goals and action steps, but inside feeling a sense of panic.

They may feel a goal sets them up for failure and so become averse to the whole process of goal setting and action planning.

- Ask people about any previous experience of setting a goal or action planning.
- Do they know what this is?
- How do they really feel about the process?

Reframe:

- Those who struggle with a concept of a future self may well be better at living in the moment, of enjoying the journey rather than obsessing about the destination.

Imagine you are going on a journey:

You put the postcode into your sat nav – you know where you are going, the route, how long it will take.

> You go into autopilot – thinking about other things, following instructions without question.

Now think about starting a journey with no sat nav, no destination.

> You're simply travelling, seeing where the road takes you, enjoying the scenery, making decisions as you go along, not worrying about arriving on time.
>
> So what if it leads to a dead end – you're happy to turn around and try another route. There is no success, no failure.
>
> You are curious, mindful, resilient and learning.

Diversify the questions

Forwards and Backwards:

Instead of 'where are you now?', 'where do you want to be?' and 'how are you going to get there?' (Egan) you could try 'what steps did you take to get to this place? What challenges did you face on the way? How did you overcome these challenges? What support and resources did you need in place? In what order did you take those steps? Which of the steps felt more enjoyable' (Hambly and Bomford). The Linear backwards approach can be used to look at plans that have already happened, or by imagining a plan has happened and using narrative to explain how that feels.

Now:

You can start with the now – ask *what?* before *why?* and *how?*

The *Good Day, Bad Day* exercise is great as a starting point for this:

- What makes a good day for you?
- What does this tell us about what matters to you?
- What makes a bad day for you?
- What does this tell us about the support you may need?

When you have a picture of a person's Good/Bad day, you can progress into planning with curious 'what if' questions:

- 'what might happen if . . .?',
- 'what could make a good day better?'

Thinking differently

The terms 'neurodivergent' and 'neurodiverse' refer to people whose thought patterns, behaviours or learning styles fall outside of what is considered the norm (or 'neurotypical').

Neurodivergence embraces the idea that differences in the human brain are natural and can lead to meaningful and positive insights and abilities.

Our brains like familiarity.

It is normal to feel anxious about change and to struggle with making decisions. Try using 'safe mode' to work out how a client can best make decisions.

- Find a safe decision the client has already made and ask them to describe how they made it.
- Consider how the same method could be applied to a more difficult decision.
- Share how you would have made the same decision but in a different way.

Maybe you would just give it a go without researching or worrying, ask other people for their thoughts, do lots of research, procrastinate . . .

Procrastinate (*verb*)

delay or postpone action; put off doing something:

- Discuss the differences – not with any intention to change how they make decisions or manage change, but to introduce awareness that there are different ways of planning and decision-making.

This can introduce options they may not have considered – perhaps taking a small step or trying something, without a goal in mind so you can get some practice in.

Triggers and blockers

We all have emotional responses to the things we do (or do not do!)

- Ask your client what makes them do something/take action, and what stops them (Triggers and Blockers).

Triggers are what make you *want* to do something, what works for you – this could be getting a reward, for example, if I finish this piece of writing before 4pm I'll have time to go swimming; it could be 'saying it out loud'. Everyone is different!

Blockers are the things that *stop* us from making a decision or carrying out a plan.

- Consider the 'blockers': What is the worst that could happen? How could that be dealt with?

Having a strategy in place for a blocker reduces anxiety – for you and the client.

In Chapter 7, Ren explained that the CDP would not be able to help them as they would not do anything they were asked to do!

This was dealt with via a suggestion of 'just one thing' . . . with the understanding that there was no expectation anything would result from it.

What is the worst that could happen? . . . Ren does nothing (so we're no worse off than now!). Someone thinks this CDP can't do their job properly (opportunity! Let's tell some more people what we actually do).

Outcome – Ren tries 'just one thing' . . . and then quite a few more things subsequently.

Here's another example of someone who didn't want a 'plan':

Punk action planning

Creating space for clients is really important, especially when they feel constrained or constricted by the education system or by the act of making a choice that is scary.

In this session, Chris was working with a Year 12 student who gets stressed by plans. ANY planning at all sent them into a tailspin.

They want a plan, not an imposed plan, yet when they plan, they feel constrained.

Chris started the session by gently agreeing to not make plans or talk about plans at all.

They were ambivalent about the future . . . university and apprenticeships were just 'ok'. They want to travel at some point in life – France and the Netherlands, and when they are 60, live in a cottage, possibly in Cornwall.

They talked about it being ok to not plan, to go with the flow; 'careers' aren't just about work but also the life we choose to lead and the choices we make . . . also the consequences of different choices.

They asked . . . 'Like whether I do a Gap Year . . . which HAS to be a year between now and starting Uni?'

Chris said: 'Or not. You could just keep on travelling.'

They were like . . . huh?

Chris was like 'yup'.

Chris said . . . 'we could just explore consequences of these different choices, but with the promise you don't have to make any choices and I won't force you to make any decisions.'

They said that was ok.

What ensued was a highly interactive career session, where they explored going to Uni in a 'traditional' application cycle, deferred entry, applying during travelling and after travelling.

They chose some coloured pens and then . . . accidentally, they started making choices about what they wanted to do and not do.

Travel.

Work.

Writing a CV. . .

When, where and how they needed help.

They action planned.

Chris stepped back and let them run with it . . . just asking questions to help gain clarity.

At the end Chris remarked, 'It looks like you made some choices. I didn't think you were going to. How do you feel about it?'

They laughed . . . and said 'It's cool. Really cool'.

When asked if this was enough or should Chris type it up they said 'nah, THIS is it! How did you do that?!'

After some discussion they agreed to call it 'punk action planning' (they were a punk and the colours matched their vibe and hair) 😎

'Action planning' happens within guidance, not as an afterthought, or some 'boxes' that are filled in.

'Action plans' can be what you make them but, must always be client centred.

If Chris had typed up a 'nice word document' as the action plan, it wouldn't have been theirs.

Do it together

- Action planning should be collaborative – revisit the section on asking questions and check you don't 'agree' action plans by asking a leading question.

Time

We all perceive time very differently – and for some the idea of looking forward to a future time is really scary.

- Talk to clients about how far ahead in time they want their action plan to go. Some people feel more secure knowing what they may be able to do at 25 or 60, others want to get this day/week over and done with before planning more.
- You don't have to flag up future options as part of a client's plan – you can provide this as a separate document that they can choose to read or ignore.

Back-up plans

In Chapter 6 we had a look at back-up plans – considering whose agenda it is to have one and how to discuss this with our clients.

If someone doesn't want one that is their choice.

An alternative to having a back-up plan is to **add value** to a current plan:

- What else could you do to improve your chances of achieving your goal?
- What can you do to ensure that if there is a gap in your plan – maybe you don't get a training place first time round – you have something to do which will improve your chances next time?

- Are there challenges you want to make? For example, some disabled people want to challenge criteria or decisions they feel are discriminatory.
- Would you like 'just one' plan now and another one added in later on?

Sharing action plans

- Discuss with clients when we start work, what information, how much and with whom we will share to ensure clients are kept at the centre of what we do.
- Also check at the end of the session if there is anything they want omitted.

During contracting Fozal said they wanted their action plan shared with school and home.

When discussing circles of support Fozal identified people who could help with different things. As part of this conversation they said: 'I won't ask Dad, he's useless'.

At the end of the session we discussed what not to write down and put a line through the note about Dad!

- Be specific on the action plan about who it is, and is not, to be shared with.

Sharing the action plan with a lead professional, and any relevant Learning Support staff, is important so they can build the client's wishes into their transition plans.

It can also be useful as a sense check, as the client might not be as aware of issues or situations that may impact on their next steps. In turn, the same can be true of sharing information with parents or carers.

Such sharing of information to ensure clients are supported requires consideration, especially if there is friction with others in their network (whether members of staff in a school or college, or even with family members).

Discussing with clients how 'sharing with others' is built into the careers support is important in providing clients with the autonomy, agency and ownership of their own lives and actions. This is crucial if the action plan will form part of the discussions at an annual or transitional review with other professionals and family members present.

- It should not be just assumed that information will be shared and that 'careers support' is something which is 'done to them' rather than with them.
- Sharing action plans with a client's circle of support is a way of extending their opportunities to explore ideas with support – but it is ultimately their choice whether to share or not.

Explain how circles of support could help:

A student with autism who was wanting to start their own bakery talked about what they were finding tricky. It turned out that they couldn't find anyone to give them business advice. As we talked it through, it turned out their aunt ran a business. The student hadn't considered asking her, as it wasn't a bakery, so for their way of thinking it wasn't obvious to ask them. As part of their plan they decided to ask their aunt for support with their business ideas.

Information sharing

As part of our code ethics, confidentiality is key, however for many clients their personal support network is important in helping them take their plans to fruition.

For many students who have additional needs their support network is going to be vital in enabling them to succeed. This awareness builds on not only Community Interaction Theory (Bill Law) which discusses where our ideas come from and who influences them but also the Systems Theory Framework of Careers Development by McMahon and Patton.

Enthusiastic consent!

For us, it is a question of building consent into the sessions, of what we will share, with whom and how.

- You could try the Open Partnership Model, which we covered in Chapter 6, but it is your choice as to what method works best for you.

We have seen some colleagues weave this sometimes-tricky element into their contracting using flash cards or posters which are prepared as prompts for discussion.

However you choose to weave it in, it is important to consider the language which is used and that it is appropriate and understandable (without being patronising) by the client group you are working with.

- If using the word 'confidential' as part of your discussion, check that the client knows what it means by asking them what they think it means.
- If they struggle with verbal communication, ask them to point to a prepared card with a simplified definition on.
- Have some examples ready, if they aren't sure.

What many of us will say is that we won't share what is discussed with anyone else, unless it affects the health and safety of the client or others (and then discuss/provide an example).

It is worth expanding this to include action plans and a discussion about what is produced, how and who it is shared with. Some of this might be included in pre-session information you have provided but, even if this is the case, it is worth 'checking-in' with the client and discussing so the understanding is explicit (rather than implicit).

Doing this protects against any issues which may arise later (such as clients not wanting to share information with others). It is an approach which is embedded in our commitment to a transparent practice (as per our CDI code of ethics).

Part of our agreement with our clients at the start of a session is about ensuring that the client's voice is heard and consents to how the client and adviser will work together.

It is important to explore whether the client is happy to share their action plan, and what is written on it, with their education setting, Learning Support team or social worker, as well as parents or carers.

> While showing them the blank action plan:
>
> 'We can add notes to the Action Plan during the session. I will then type it up neatly after the session and send it on to your tutor so, they can support with your next steps.
>
> However, if you tell me, you don't like your teacher, I won't write it on your Action Plan.'
>
> 'And if you don't want it sent to your tutor let me know where else to send it.'

For most clients this isn't an issue.

Occasionally clients raise concerns about what is shared. This can be easily resolved by having some back-up solutions available.

- One option is to have a separate piece of paper or pre-printed 'manual/paper action plan' document available.

You can agree to write on these things for just the client, with the typed action plan kept 'for the school' only containing that which the client is happy to share with others.

- Another option is to discuss what concerns they might have and type the whole action plan up with the client – agreeing on the wording together – so, when it is shared, they are ok with what has been written.
- It is important to check why the client doesn't wish to share the information with others in case it links with a child protection or safeguarding concern (in which case, this takes precedence over the clients' wishes).

For many of our clients with additional needs there is a tension between the action plan being a client-led process and a document written to support local authority transitions to post-16/19 options.

To resolve this potential conflict it is important that the approach to action planning is agreed before delivery, to avoid misunderstandings around expectations.

We need to be mindful that some of the most client-centred ways of working don't always align with the formal requirements of some Local Authorities, schools, colleges or funders.

Different practitioners will have varying approaches and (depending on the organisation or contract area you work for) you may have some very specific guidelines you will be working within, which will affect not only what you write but also how much and for whom.

It might be that you don't have the leeway to make your action plans more inclusive (by changing fonts and colours), but do ask your organisation about this.

- What can you do in your practice to make your delivery more inclusive; not just for clients but also colleagues?

Inclusive approaches to action planning

Action plan formats (inclusive by design)
If we are to strive as a society to remove the barriers our clients contend with, it is crucial we start with how our own work attends to this.

Here's an example from the Young Peoples' Service at CXK.

A member of staff has dyslexia which impacts not only on their ability to read and process information but also their organisational skills and use of spreadsheets.

CXK discussed their needs and how dyslexia manifested for them.

CXK researched 'Inclusive by Design' principles, with an ambition to embed these into the overall design of tools and processes.

Inclusive by design

This description by Val Querini is useful:

> Inclusive design is the practice of intentionally including the needs of users who likely experience exclusion in many aspects of their daily lives due to being part of an oppressed group or a statistical minority. If we don't intentionally include the risk is to unintentionally exclude.

Their writing goes further, stating:

> People with disabilities, oppressed minorities, and potentially any user (ourselves included) can and do experience exclusion when interacting with a digital product. Negative, exclusionary, and discriminatory user experiences come in many forms, including:
>
> - Denied access
> - Identity demeaning experiences
> - Unwanted exposure of sensitive information (real or perceived)
> - Frustrating experiences

Taking this into consideration, one way we can define an inclusive design approach is to say that it should enable the delivery of solutions that are not just easy to access, but also make people feel welcomed, safe, and valued.

- Val's article – follow the link in the resources section – provides a host of useful links and is a useful primer for this way of thinking and working.

In supporting a colleague these are the key elements CXK developed:

- All record-keeping spreadsheets (where CXK track clients they have worked with) are dark purple on a buff background and use a larger clearer font (Century Gothic, 12+).

They decided on this after talking to a range of experts at universities, SENCOs across various schools and colleges, gaining client feedback (regarding action plans), as well as researching online and using online guides.

- Black on white was seen to be the least favourable for readability overall.
- They considered visually impaired readers and needed a design which catered for as many individuals as possible.
- Action plan templates (typed and pre-printed ones on paper) are now all created on a buff background and use Century Gothic, size 12. This enables clients who have Dyslexia, Colour Blindness or Impaired Vision to access them more easily.
- An action plan template was created to enable colleagues to reduce the amount of writing they were doing for each client and used boxes for options which can be deleted as appropriate.
- On their YouTube channel aimed at clients and other professionals, they ensure that subtitles are added as a 'default' setting.

This has helped:

- reduce stress levels;
- increase confidence; and
- enable Chris' dyslexic colleague to deliver with greater professionalism.

Their reflection on the changes:

> For the first time, I can pick up any document and just read it. In all my years I've never had this . . . it's just removed a massive barrier and made things easier . . . I have never felt more accepted and supported.

A few relatively easy adjustments can make a huge difference in the work place.

Consider what difference some changes can make for our clients!

Colours matter

We were aware that Cat used a colour overlay for much of their work.

When it came to the action plan we asked them what colour they would like the background and font (as well as what type of font).

We played around with it together until they were happy.

Cat selected a 'rose coloured background with a dark blue Arial font, size 12'.

The look on their face was one of relief once we had done this.

We then also talked about how much we would write on the action plan to avoid Cat becoming overwhelmed.

We typed the action plan together (after offering them the option to type it, if they wished).

The final action plan was one where 'less was definitely more'. It

- Had information which was well spaced out.
- Was in colours and a font which worked for Cat.
- Used bullets to highlight key points.
- Used **bold text** to **highlight keywords** and the **terminology** they wished to remember.
- Used the highlight function for the embedded *hyperlinks* we added to make it quick and easy to navigate to the online information from the session.

How did that make Cat feel?

'accepted, included and supported, without being judged'

CXK are now working on a digital action plan template which can sit on a laptop or tablet with pre-filled criteria, generated in an inclusive format.

- Learn how to change the background colours, font colours and styles on your digital action plans to make these more accessible when working with clients.
- Share and discuss the accessibility settings within Windows, Apple and Chromebook so staff are confident how to access these.

Free 'inclusive by design' poster resources are also available on the CXK website.

Person-centred planning

Person-centred planning aims to put children and young people at the centre of planning and decisions that affect them. When children are meaningfully involved, this can change their attitude, behaviour and learning and make them active partners who work with adults to bring about change.

A model of person-centred planning aims to:

- put children and young people at the centre of planning and decisions that affect them;
- bring people together – both to celebrate successes and also to address difficulties with honesty and care;
- help children and young people learn how to express their views, how to choose and how to listen;
- show children and young people that they are listened to, respected and valued and cared for – that they belong;
- help adults get to know the children and young people they work with, and give insight into the impact they are having on children and young people;
- make plans that build towards meaningful outcomes for children and young people and their families.

You may be asked by a parent or a young person to attend a Person-Centred Planning meeting.

- Person-Centred Planning is not just for people with a learning disability – it is a helpful approach for many people.
- The NDTi host a range of information and resources from the Preparing for Adulthood programme including Person-Centred Planning tools. Also, have a look at the resources available from the Careers Enterprise Company and Careers Services in Scotland, Wales and Northern Ireland. Links are in our resources section.
- Just because a resource was made in Scotland doesn't mean it can't be used in Wales. Simply avoid any that have specific pathways detailed on them.

PATH, MAPS and circles

PATH
Planning **A**lternative **T**omorrows with **H**ope

PATH was developed by John O'Brien, Marsha Forest and Jack Pearpoint.

It is a graphical model for planning that helps people find direction and build strength.

People can use PATH when they:

- are stuck and have nothing to look forward to;
- have people who care about them but don't know how to help;
- have a sense of a better future, but need help to say what it is;

- like the idea of a planning event for themselves and their circle of support.

PATH starts with:

- The Dream – Always start with the dream, also known as the North Star.

It then looks at:

- The Goal – possible positive outcomes.
- Now – a description of how the client thinks and feels about current situations.
- Enrolment – All the people in the room are invited to sign up and make a commitment to the PATH.
- Stronger – What are the things we need to keep us strong and motivate us to keep up our commitment to the PATH?
- Next steps.
- Feelings – everybody says in one word how they are feeling right now.

MAPS
Map **A**ction **P**lanning **S**ystem

MAPS was developed by John O'Brien, Marsha Forest, Jack Pearpoint, Judith Snow and David Hasbury.

It asks a series of questions which individuals can use to develop a plan of action to head towards their dream and away from the nightmare.

People can use MAPS when:

- they need to see where they have been in the past to see where they are going next;
- they want people to recognise their gifts and strengths;
- they want people to understand their fears.

How MAPS works?

- It is a group exercise for the client and their circle of support.
- The person tells their 'story' and why they are here.
- They can describe situations past and present.
- If this is difficult the person can nominate someone to tell their story.
- The story is recorded and then agreed by the person. This will allow the person to tell the story once.

The *dream* is an opportunity for the person to say what they want to change about their life and express what their aspirations, hopes and dreams are.

The *nightmare* is their fears and worries in preparing for the dream.

The circle of support then supports the person by identifying and listing their gifts, strengths and talents.

They think about the best way to move forward towards the dream and away from the nightmare for the person.

Jointly they develop the action plan, listing who will do what, where and when.

4 +1 Questions
We can use *4 + 1 Questions* when:

- a gentle, collaborative approach is needed;
- people in the client's life are stuck and don't know what to try next with them;
- lots of different approaches have been tried with little success.

How 4+1 Questions work?
Set out sheets of paper which are headed with the following questions:-

1. What's been tried?
2. What we've learnt?
3. What we are pleased about?
4. What we are concerned about?
5. Based on what we know what should we do next?

The 4 + 1 Questions are a quick way to work out better ways of supporting people, and supporters are less likely to focus on the 'what-are-we-concerned-about' list. This method can also be used as a way to conduct an interim or follow-up review.

Cloud map

If producing a cloud map of ideas as an 'action plan' as part of the careers session, capture these as a poster.

Email a photo of it to your client or get them to take a photo with their mobile phone (so ideas aren't lost if the poster is damaged or mislaid).

You can copy in a member of staff too with agreement.

Within your email or message, provide a brief explanation and any suggested next steps which have been agreed in the session.

- Within this approach, there is a blurring between the poster being a document from the session and the email becoming an action plan in itself, which is worth reflecting on and being mindful of.
- If using props as part of the guidance session and action planning, sometimes in conjunction with cards and/or sticky notes, taking a photo is a really easy way of capturing ideas for the future (similar to the poster but in three dimensions!)
- There are risks with this approach, that the 'formal' action plan becomes a document which is taken more seriously by other professionals supporting the client and/or can become wordier and owned less by the client.

We would encourage you to consider how you can make your action plans more inclusive and client centred.

Ask yourself some questions:

- Can the clients I am working with make sense of the format?
- Does the action plan fulfil multiple purposes? For example, is it for use by the client and local authority or education provider?
- How accessible is it?
- Does it need to be adjusted to become more accessible or meaningful for your client(s)?
- Have you asked the client what format they prefer?

The resources section has links to lots of further information and tools to add to your toolkit. You can access it via the QR code and URL at the start of the book.

For some explanation about different impairments, and some of the words and phrases used within learning support and disability communities, have a look at our glossary.

Chapter 10
Using theory in our practice

In the context of Careers – whether within a group setting or 1:1 guidance – we draw on our knowledge and understanding of **Career Theory** to underpin our practice.

You may already be familiar with the many different Career Theories. If not, we've listed a few sources in our resources section to help you learn.

Both of us use combinations of different theories when working with clients in order to personalise our work to suit how they think and learn.

In this chapter, we won't be examining all the theories in depth, but instead we'll look at why some may work better than others for an individual, and where theories from other disciplines are useful in Careers work. We will provide a brief descriptor for the theories we mention but won't cover them all (some of our colleagues already do this, so please do follow their work).

Over time, the shift has been from 'positivist' theories, where the individual is seen as a rational decision-maker, to 'constructivist' approaches based on the idea of a complex individual creating their own reality within their social context.

A brief look at some career theories:

Differentialism

People search for environments where they can use their skills and abilities and express their values and attitudes: Realistic, Investigative, Artistic, Social, Enterprising, Conventional.

This theory is reflected in personality or job matching tests such as the ones you find on the National Careers Service website.

Reflections:

'Work' is defined within this as doing things to achieve a purpose, like paid and unpaid jobs, volunteering, sports or hobbies.

So, it does not make the assumption that 'careers' is simply about getting paid work. Some disabled people we work with may not engage in paid work for a variety of reasons. However, learning the skills to make choices and plan can be life-changing . . . so we should not exclude people from Career Guidance simply because others presume they will never work.

Personality or job matching tests are simplistic and do not take into account the disabling factors that affect us.

Some can also require metaphorical thinking (the Buzz quiz, for example, links you to an animal). If you are a literal thinker, this can seem nonsensical.

Developmentalism

Recognised that people weren't fixed quantities but developed and matured over time; that decision-making was a lifelong process reflecting different stages in life.

For example, Super's developmental theory considers the importance of exploration as part of growing our 'opportunity awareness' and 'decision making', as well as other key elements relating to how we maintain and develop our careers:

Reflections:

The *roles* do not reflect many aspects of some disabled people's lives – there is no recognition of differences in the development and experience of society.

The theory does promote 'work-life balance' and the concept that people change over time.

The timelines which Ginzberg and Super align with their fantasy and explorative phases coincide with the latest understanding regarding the teenage brain and the prefrontal cortex and how this affects decision-making. Some of the latest research on neurodivergent conditions indicates a delay in the development of the prefrontal cortex; from this, we might argue that neurodivergent people may remain longer in the 'fantasy and explorative' phases (closer to their early 30s rather than mid-20s). Research in this area is limited.

For older adults or people who have a degenerative condition, for example, the onset of brain degeneration will affect their ability to formulate career plans and make decisions. It is important for us as practitioners to grow our understanding of the various conditions our clients will have and how these affect career planning and their career management. Reading beyond the 'careers sphere' is vital to ensure we remain informed.

There is debate around the effects that nature, nurture and culture may have on what we consider the developmental stages. (Aspects of

Bill Law's community interaction theory touch upon this.) This theory is worth being aware of in our work supporting disabled clients, as there is a risk we will collude with social norms and, in doing so, be complicit in closing off opportunities for our clients.

Other commentators, such as Gideon Arulmani, also consider the very idea of a 'career' a cultural construct;[1] therefore, we must be wary of applying predominantly Western definitions of what a 'career' is or isn't and whether the life stages we discuss in career theories are inherent to everyone or purely a social construct found within recent Western cultures.

Structuralism

'Structural' barriers mean that many people cannot access opportunities and therefore their career options are limited. These barriers either need to be overcome through social change or mitigated by building the capacity of individuals.

Reflections:

Being able to 'succeed' despite 'disadvantages' is very much a Charity model of disability (see Chapter 3).

Envisioning a future of limited opportunity does not encourage personal aspiration or creative thinking for many.

The theory does, however, recognise that barriers exist, which opens up the opportunity to discuss and address these.

Social Learning

Theorists aim to integrate structure and agency. They focus more on the importance of the process of learning, how it influences what we learn and the ability to succeed through persistence (Krumbolz, Law, Bandura).

Reflections:

Using a more holistic approach is useful with many people – their relationship to the world they live in is taken into account.

The idea that if we simply keep trying, we will eventually be able to do something is not the experience of many disabled people. We often need to try doing something differently . . . or doing something different.

The DOTS Model by Tony Law and Bill Watts from 1977 considers the different stages individuals need to attend to while career planning. The longstanding meme of rearranging the letters into 'SOD iT' remains a useful way of remembering the different stages of DOTS being: Self, Opportunities, Decisions and Transitions

Reflections:

Originally designed as a way to analyse research findings, it remains a useful lens through which to consider an institution's careers programme and the extent to which it meets the needs of those who attend it.

It also remains a useful tool to enable a client to consider their own career management and what they may need to do at each stage to help them to move forward.

The complexity of our interactions with the world was not overtly considered.

DOTS was reviewed and expanded in the 1990s by Bill Law to reflect the increasingly complex and changeable nature of work by adding a contextual layer, which considers the subjective nature of how clients see the world. Called the SeSiFU model, it attended to clients' Sensing, Sifting, Focusing and Understanding at each stage of DOTS.

Reflections:

This contextual layer is a useful reminder for us to make sure we consider what the world looks like from the clients' perspective (regardless of our own understanding of a situation or that of the client's 'professionals', parents, carers or teachers).

It is the client's own viewpoint which is paramount, as they are the one who has to live with the decisions they are making and the life they are constructing. It reminds us to ensure we are truly capturing the client's thoughts, ideas and voice in our work.

'Planned Happenstance' and 'Chaos'

Theories suggest that our ability to control events is limited, but we can 'plan' for unpredictability by developing our networks and connections, building our skills and being open to opportunities when they arise.

Reflections:

The focus shifts from devising long-term career plans to the development of career management skills, which may suit people who struggle to envisage their 'future self', as many autistic people do.

The concept of Chaos can be off-putting for people who enjoy order and routine.

Individuals are seen as their own expert and the careers development professional's role is to help the client create their own 'narrative'.

Emotional, social and cultural impact are considered as part of career planning.

> Career Inaction theory looks at:
> - difficulties in making decisions;
> - anxiety about uncertain outcomes;
> - short-term costs winning over long-term gains;
> - cognitive overload/stress.
>
> Reflections:
>
> We are encouraged to consider *why* people may have difficulty implementing decisions. This prompts us to relate to a person in a very holistic way and recognise their individual barriers to inclusion.
>
> It encompasses a range of techniques which can be particularly useful for people who are disabled by society; for example, transformational coaching, motivational interviewing, inspirational stories of other people who were in a similar situation and having a mentor or role model who can support them through the transition.

What other theory can be helpful?

Social pedagogy describes a holistic, person-centred way of working with people across the course of their lives . . .

It addresses social inequality and facilitates change by nurturing learning, wellbeing and connection at an individual and community level.

It promotes wellbeing, learning and growth and seeks to recognise individual potential.

There is an expectation that individuals are supported to identify and design support that enhances their wellbeing.

> Meaning of **pedagogy** in English (noun)
> *the study of the methods and activities of teaching*
> *Cambridge dictionary*

Reflections:

Much of the practice around 'person-centred planning' (which is cited as best practice within learning support processes) comes from Social Pedagogy. It is not often examined as 'Career Theory' but is used widely as an approach by Careers professionals working in Learning Support settings.

Practitioners are encouraged to recognise that nothing is fixed when we enter the lives of others, so we draw upon what we feel is required to engage in a given context. This helps us work in a more creative, flexible and person-centred way.

We may (as a carer, careers practitioner or support worker) struggle with person-centred approaches when we feel the individual is not making choices that are in their best interests. Our section on Mental Capacity looks at 'unwise choices'!

> Wellbeing as a concept has taken centre stage in adult social care narratives. The Care Act (2014) and subsequent policies have cemented this notion, promoting a strength-based approach to social care.

Sensory integration theory

From a health services perspective, this intersects with autism treatment. It is common for individuals with autism to experience atypical responses to sensory experiences. Interventions that are based on sensory integration theories are founded on the notion that these responses are due to difficulties modulating sensory information (Whitney, 2018).

Reflections:

The underpinning research has given a wealth of insight into the way sensory processing affects our ability to communicate, relate to people and environments, process information and use executive functioning. This can be exceptionally helpful to understand when clients are perceiving the world very differently from ourselves (see Chapter 2).

There is currently limited reported evidence for the effectiveness of interventions based on sensory integration theory as a whole – and it is based on the premise that people need to 'improve participation in daily occupations', which may not be what the individual wants or needs.

Play theory

Play theory generally refers to cognitive development in children.

As children play, they are exploring the world around them, learning about themselves and others, building language and literacy skills, role-playing situations to find solutions and learning to regulate their behaviour. Self-directed play can be active (running around the playground on a bike path), quiet (looking at a book or cradling a doll) or a combination (trying on a parent's shoes and trying to walk in them).

- The amount of time children spend in uninterrupted self-directed play – when no one is teaching them and they are free to decide what and how to play – has declined tremendously in educational settings and in the home lives of children. Disabled children have even less opportunity than their non-disabled peers to engage in self-directed play, resulting in little chance of learning the skills they need for successful career planning and decision-making.

> **Loose parts for children with diverse abilities**
>
> Loose parts play is the active, joyful way children choose to spend their time when they are not directed by adults. It is also how children, regardless of their ability or background, connect with one another.
>
> Every person, object and space design is interconnected, each affecting the other. In an inclusive ecosystem, children are not only present but are considered active and valuable members of the family, school and community. When we approach education from an ecosystem perspective, we begin to value beauty in humans and their surroundings as a catalyst for transforming children's lives.
>
> – Miriam Beloglovsky | November 2022

Play is not just for children. If we are to offer the opportunity for our clients to develop problem-solving skills, language, collaboration, and to show increased attention to processes, structures and outcomes we can use play principles within our work.

In recent years, *serious games* and other game frameworks have emerged as a tool for teaching. Game-based learning involves integrating effective teaching and learning with the features of games, such as interactive storytelling, problem-solving challenges and immersive environments, to create engaging and compelling learning experiences.

The use of play-based learning in Careers is increasing – take a look at *CareersCraft on Minecraft* as an example.

Our 'Relate' Model

Ok, so this isn't technically a 'theory', but we thought we'd explain what we do to embed and use theory, and lived experience, within our work.

Writing a book on career guidance techniques and approaches to use with those who are 'disabled' or have 'additional needs' is an interesting concept. When you really start thinking about it, we could say that everyone has 'individual needs'. What makes the needs 'additional' is how society fails to address these needs.

Yet do 'traditional' approaches address the needs of the majority either? And what do we mean by 'traditional' anyway?

The approaches we talk about in this book aren't exclusively for those with learning or additional needs and can be utilised with neurotypical and non-disabled individuals. With careers guidance driven primarily as a client-centred process, meeting the 'individual needs' of each person we work with is vital.

Many people are unfamiliar with our profession and may not understand the differences between Careers Education, Information, Advice and Guidance.

The key areas of career development work are described here by the CDI:

- Careers Education: Usually in educational settings, this refers to a range of actions to educate people on the potential careers available, develop career management skills and explore their own career potential.
- Career information: Providing information, such as different job roles or the local labour market, to help clients make informed decisions.
- Career advice: Offering guidance on the different pathways based on the client's needs, goals and situation.
- Career guidance: Career coaching helps the client explore their own strengths and development needs, aspirations, barriers and needs, so the client has the self-understanding to confidently define their next steps.

Chris recalls talking to a colleague when he worked as a visiting careers adviser with construction, motor vehicle and electrical students.

'Don't you get bored, having the same conversation with each student doing the same course?' they asked.

'Not in the least – I don't have the same conversation with each student; I get to know each student, their hopes, dreams and motivations, as well as fears; we build our sessions together from there.'

This seemed to surprise Chris' colleague!

We should approach each client with the understanding that they have 'individual needs' whether or not they have a recognised disability or additional needs.

And make sure clients and colleagues are aware of the difference between giving information and advice, and supporting people with guidance.

Jules sometimes explains the 'guidance' concept to people as 'finding out how you and your brain work . . . and using this to make sure you don't miss out on things you might be interested in'.

We try to tailor our approaches to meet the needs of each individual where we find them, rather than where we imagine them to be or wish they were. We hope you find this book useful for all of your clients.

> See what works for each individual – every person is different and will **relate** differently to things we say or do, and to the world we exist in.

Within an individual's career planning journey, these relationships can influence their perception of opportunities and barriers.

The relationship between the career development professional and their perception of the world is part of this (check out Chapter 6).

As individuals experience how others relate to them, and how the world 'feels' for them, they develop ideas about what is possible . . . and what is not.

For many disabled people, this is particularly impactful.

- If others continually focus on what you can't do, how does this affect aspiration?
- If doing activities your non-disabled peers seem to do with ease (e.g. 'chatting') takes up all your energy, where do you find the resources to explore and try other things?
- What do the limitations imposed on you by education, family and society in general do to your opportunities to check out and implement career ideas?
- When others 'label' you, what does this do?
- If your CDP is anxious about interactions with you, do you get the best guidance?

Our model encourages reflection on our part in other people's career planning experiences and their perception of the world.

> Regulate, Relate and Communicate
>
> Celebrate, Advocate and Navigate
>
> Evaluate, Investigate and Collaborate
>
> Activate, Accommodate and Create

There are many models of career planning and management.

As practitioners, awareness of these should form part of our continual professional development as we seek out alternative perspectives.

How to develop your own 'model':

- Do you like to read? Is audio more your thing? Are you a scroll-and-click person? Do videos hit home more than the written word? Enjoy doing training? Do conferences inspire you? **Engage** with continual professional development and learn from others.
- **Know your theories** and keep up to date with new thinking. We don't have to stick to one theory – use the parts that work for the individual. And explore theories that aren't labelled as 'Careers'.
- **Don't be afraid** to try out different approaches and strategies – we can be very open about this with clients. If we are not sure whether a strategy will work or not, we can simply ask permission to try it. Whether something does, or does not, work we have learnt a valuable piece of information about that individual and ourselves.
- **Share** your experiences with others. It is useful to share things that went well and things that didn't. It helps all of us expand our toolkit and develop new ideas.
- **Don't be restricted** by your environment – we don't have to 'sit and talk' even though this is the traditional perception of career guidance. It works for lots of people, but for those who need something different . . . try something different.
- **Develop your own toolkit**. In addition to strategies around talking and listening, you can create your own sensory toolkit.
- **Demonstrate** to our clients that career learning can be FUN, challenging, empowering, revelatory and life-changing . . .
- **Ask,** don't assume. Be curious. Find out how others experience the world. Embrace difference.

The resources section has links to lots of further information and tools to add to your toolkit. You can access it via the QR code and URL at the start of the book.

For some explanations about different impairments, and some of the words and phrases used within learning support and disability communities, have a look at our glossary.

Note

1 Gideon Arulmani. 'The Cultural Preparation Process Model and Career Development'. In: *Handbook of Career Development* (pp. 81–103). The Promise Foundation.

Chapter 11
Legislate and advocate

Policy and legislation

Lots of policy and legislation affects our work and the lives of the clients we work with.

We have picked out some in this chapter and offered a brief description with links in the resources section to find out more if you want.

- We do not need to be legal experts; however, if we are adopting a 'rights-based' approach to our work it is useful to know about the legislation and codes of practice that affect the lives of our clients.

Equality and discrimination

The Equality Act is probably the best-known piece of legislation which protects disabled people in the UK.

The Equality Act 2010 applies to England, Wales and Scotland. Most of the Act does not apply to Northern Ireland. Northern Ireland uses Section 75 of the Northern Ireland Act.

Scotland's equality legislation includes the Equality Act 2010 (Specific Duties) (Scotland) Regulations 2012.

Under the **Equality Act** 'disability' is defined as:

> a physical or mental impairment that has a substantial and long-term adverse effect on a person's ability to do normal daily activities.

As a disabled person, you have rights to protect you from discrimination. These rights cover most areas including:

- employment;
- education;
- dealing with the police.

Nobody has to tell their employer they're disabled. But when they do, the employer has a legal responsibility to support them. It's up to the person to decide when they want to tell their employer. Some people might choose to do this when something changes, for example, their condition starts affecting them much more than it used to.

An employer has the same legal responsibility if they could reasonably be expected to know someone is disabled, even if the person has not told them.

Employers also have a responsibility to consider whether anyone might have a disability that puts them at a disadvantage at work. This does not mean asking intrusive questions. Employers should focus on the support they can give.

The Equality Act and the United Nations (UN) Convention on disability rights help to enforce, protect and promote your rights.

The Equality Act 2010 doesn't apply to Northern Ireland which uses two pieces of legislation: Disability Discrimination Act 1995 and Special Educational Needs and Disability (NI) Order 2005.

- If you're looking for a great resource to support people to challenge discrimination, try the *Right to Participate* website.
- Rights-based organisations, like Disability Rights UK, offer Information and support, build and engage in the Disability Rights movement, create opportunities for feedback and co-production, and advocate for change.
- Think about what Equality and Equity mean.

Equality means each individual or group of people is given the same resources or opportunities.

Equity recognises that each person has different circumstances, and allocates the exact resources and opportunities needed to reach an equal outcome.

Mental capacity

The decision-making rights of people over the age of 16 in the British Isles are governed by a range of laws which all adhere to similar principles.

England or Wales – Mental Capacity Act 2005

Scotland – Adults with Incapacity (Scotland) Act 2000

Northern Ireland – Mental Capacity Act (Northern Ireland) 2016

There is an assumption that a person has capacity unless there is a reasonable belief that they do not, at which point an assessment of capacity should take place.

Mental capacity is assessed in relation to the particular decision which needs to be made. This means that whether a person has mental capacity to make a particular decision or not has to be considered on an individual basis in the light of the circumstances at the time.

Before someone can make a decision for you, they need to have a reasonable belief that you no longer have the capacity to make that decision yourself. This means asking questions like:

- Do you have a general understanding of what decisions need to be made?
- Do you have a general understanding of the consequences of the decision?
- Do you show this general understanding in the way you behave and make decisions?

If a person has capacity to **make a decision** they do not need to make a **wise decision.**

Our role, as career development professionals, is to ensure we support people to:

- understand (offering information in a way they can access it);
- make their own decisions wherever possible;
- and communicate those decisions.

You can use the Mental Capacity principles in a very proactive way – making sure disabled adults are aware they have rights.

Consider where these rights may not be made apparent . . .

- Do any of your settings invite others (parents, carers, support workers) to careers interventions without offering this as a choice to the individual?
- Do action plans get sent to others without this being the client's choice?
- Are people making 'best interest' decisions for a client even where they have capacity to make the decision themselves?
- How is decision-making explained to people?

Jo is 25 years old.

They are in their final year at an Independent Specialist College.

When we talked about future 'choices' they explained they had 'always been told to say *yes* to everything'.

This has resulted in:

- no real practice in making choices;
- feeling they are not trusted to make decisions;
- others making decisions FOR them;
- confusion about why saying 'no' is not allowed or seen as difficult behaviour;
- being made to feel like a child;
- not accessing opportunities independently;
- being potentially unsafe (the ability to say *no* is a fundamental element of safeguarding yourself).

We selected a choice that Jo wanted to make. Just one thing to start with as they were very nervous and excited . . . in this instance volunteering.

We set out a plan of action – involving their circle of support – to start practising making choices.

We did not cover all the choices available, we did not cover all their interests and skills, in fact we did not do many of the things normally covered in a careers interview. What we did was pick the thing that was most affecting Jo's ability to engage in career planning and work out how we could change this.

Jo's feedback was:

- that they were super happy;
- if they can make their own choices, and know who they can ask for help when they need it, they can start living a happy independent life;
- and no thanks to any more information because this is enough for now.

Mental capacity and learning support

The rights of young people are broadly similar across our four nations.

In England

Specific decision-making rights about Education Health and Care (EHC) plans apply to young people directly from the end of compulsory school age.

These are the right to:

- request an assessment for an EHC plan;
- make representations about the content of their EHC plan;
- request that a particular institution is named in their EHC plan;
- request a personal budget for elements of their EHC plan;
- appeal to the first-tier tribunal (SEND and Disability) about decisions concerning their EHC plan.

In Scotland

Rights of children and young people with additional support needs are covered in *Additional support for learning: guidance on assessing capacity and considering wellbeing.*

My Rights My Say is a children's service supporting children aged 12–15 to use their rights. They provide advice and information, advocacy support, legal representation and a service to independently seek children's views about the support they receive with their learning.

In Wales

There is a guide to help understand issues surrounding young people or parents of children who lack capacity in the ALN system.

If someone lacks capacity to make a decision:

- a 'best interest' decision can be made;
- an Independent Mental Capacity Advocate (IMCA) can be appointed to act on their behalf.

> When we are trying to decide whether a child or young person under the age of 16 is mature enough to make decisions for themselves, we refer to Gillick Competence and the Fraser Guidelines, which is based on a child being able to understand a decision, what it involves and to retain the information and communicate their decision.

Safeguarding

Studies have shown that disabled children are 3.8 times more likely to be neglected or physically abused, 3.1 times more likely to be sexually abused and 3.9 times more likely to be emotionally abused. In fact, findings show that 31% of disabled children suffer abuse compared with 9% of the non-disabled child population. Further to this, disabled children are also at a higher risk of experiencing multiple abuses and of enduring multiple episodes of abuse.

Why?
- Some disabled children may not recognise the abuse.
- Disabled children might not be able to ask for help.
- The child may rely on their abuser to meet their needs – making it even more difficult to speak out.
- Parents and professionals may miss signs of abuse/neglect, mistaking them as part of a child's condition.
- Professionals working with disabled children may not be trained to spot the signs of abuse and neglect.
- Children with disabilities and their families may feel isolated or without support due to a limited number of accessible services, meaning they may not know where to find help.
- Abusers may try to excuse their behaviour, blaming it on the difficulties of caring for a disabled child.
- Professionals who work to support parents' ability to meet their child's additional needs may overlook parental behaviours that are not adequate.
- Child protection professionals might not have the specialised skills to properly communicate with the child, or to accurately assess or understand a disabled child's needs.

The way abuse is reported for children and adults at risk is not the same and the legislation for managing each is different.

How do you (or your organisation) make sure everyone understands the right steps to take when they're worried someone is not safe?

All adults, including adults at risk, have a right to make unwise decisions – including the choice not to take action to protect themselves. This is different for children, where their safety is the primary concern – although listening to their views is still important.

When you're safeguarding adults, you must consider the individual adult's needs in every situation. This might include considering whether the adult is subject to coercion or undue influence.

Human rights

The European Convention on Human Rights (ECHR) has been incorporated into UK domestic law through the Human Rights Act 1998 (HRA). Everyone, including children and young people, has these rights, no matter what their circumstances. Under international law, States/Governments are obliged to respect, protect and fulfil human rights. Those delivering public services should respect human rights when they make decisions, plan services and make policies.

Advocacy

Some clients may want, or need, an advocate.

Advocacy means getting support from another person to help you express your views and wishes, and helping you stand up for your rights.

This is a specific role – and has a distinct skillset.

The principles of advocacy are:

- clarity of purpose;
- safeguard confidentiality;
- equality and diversity;
- empowerment;
- putting people first.

There are various pieces of legislation which provide rights to advocacy services and some organisations offer wider services to disabled people. You can find advocacy services on Local Authority websites.

Learning support, transition and preparing for adulthood

In England

The Children and Families Act 2014 makes provision about children, families and people with special educational needs or disabilities; to make provision about the right to request flexible working; and for connected purposes.

It extends to England and Wales only, and applies to England only. The significant exceptions are explained in the links labelled *Children and Families Act 2014 Territorial Extent and Application* in the resources section.

The SEND Code of Practice explains the duties of local authorities, health bodies, schools and colleges to provide for those with special educational needs under part 3 of the Children and Families Act 2014. The Children Act 1989 sets out the responsibilities of local authorities towards looked-after children and care leavers.

In Scotland

The Education (Additional Support for Learning) (Scotland) Act 2004 sets out duties and *Additional support for learning: statutory guidance 2017* provides guidance on all aspects of the 2004 Act and is a code of practice for education authorities.

As part of the Principles into Practice Trial, ARC Scotland developed an online tool called Compass. Compass helps young people, parents and carers, and professionals understand the transitions process better and find useful information at the right time. It is free of charge and can be used in all areas of Scotland to help prepare and plan for transitions.

ARC Scotland works alongside people who need additional support, and their families. This includes people with learning disabilities, autism, mental health difficulties, sensory or physical disabilities.

In Wales

The additional learning needs (ALN) system is the new system for supporting children and young people aged 0 to 25 with ALN. The ALN system is replacing the special educational learning needs (SEN) system and the system for supporting young people with learning difficulties and/or disabilities (LDD).

The ALN legislative framework is created by the *Additional Learning Needs and Education Tribunal (Wales) Act 2018 (the ALN Act), the Additional Learning Needs Code for Wales 2021 (the ALN Code) and regulations made under the Act.*

In Northern Ireland

The SEN Code of Practice (1998) is statutory guidance based on the *Education Order (Northern Ireland) 1996 and The Education (SEN) Regulations 2005.*

The Education Order (Northern Ireland) 1996 provides the current definitions for SEN and SEN Provision.

The Care Act (England and Wales) focuses on adults with care and support needs and was implemented in April 2015.

If a child is likely to have needs when they turn 18, their local authority should carry out an assessment before then to determine what these will be.

Statutory guidance suggests that these assessments take place when it is easier to understand what the needs of the child and carer will be beyond the age of 18.

For most children it is likely that they will take place during the transition process, from around age 14.

Telling others about an impairment or health condition

There is no legislation saying that people need to disclose a disability.

Some reasons why they might not . . .

1. concerns that this will have a negative impact on their application;
2. previous experience of discrimination;
3. concerns about confidentiality;
4. lack of awareness that their condition would fall under the heading of disability.

Some good reasons to share:

- Identifying as disabled gives you protection under the Equality Act 2010.
- This enables you to access specialist support and adjustments – for study and for work.
- Although it might be unfamiliar or uncomfortable to use the term for the first time, remember that disability is about the barriers created by society.
- It is not about your worth, ability or intellect.

In our resources section we have put links to legislation, support agencies and guidance for England, Northern Ireland, Scotland and Wales.

Glossary

Glossary – *'an alphabetical list, with meanings, of the words or phrases in a text that are difficult to understand'*

In our glossary, we have included some descriptions of impairments and some of the words and phrases used within learning support and disability communities.

The resources section has links to lots of further information. You can access it via the QR code and URL at the start of the book.

A

Academy
An academy is a school that receives funding directly from the government and is not controlled by the local authority.

Activities of daily living (ADL)
Basic self-care tasks that must be accomplished every day, such as eating, bathing, dressing, toileting, transferring and continence.

ADD, ADHD\C and AuDHD
Attention Deficit Disorder, Attention Deficit and Hyperactivity Disorder and Autism and Attention and Hyperactivity Disorder.

The symptoms of attention deficit (hyperactivity) disorder can be categorised into two types of behaviour:

- inattentiveness (difficulty concentrating and focusing) and
- hyperactivity and impulsiveness.

Many people with ADHD have problems that fall into both these categories, but this is not always the case.

Some people with the condition have problems with concentration and focusing, but not with hyperactivity or impulsiveness.

This is known as attention deficit disorder (ADD). ADD can sometimes go unnoticed because the symptoms may be less obvious.

ADHD is more often diagnosed in boys than girls. Girls are more likely to have symptoms of inattentiveness only and are less likely to show disruptive behaviour that makes symptoms more obvious. This means girls who have AD(H)D may not always be diagnosed.

AuDHD is gaining in popularity as a term, especially as a nonclinical definition of need, among teenagers and twenty-somethings.

Some people with ADHD prefer to substitute the last D of Disorder for C, for Condition.

https://embrace-autism.com/an-introduction-to-audhd/

Additional education needs (AEN)
This relates to children or young people who face additional barriers to their learning, which makes it difficult for them to achieve their full potential.

These needs range and can include:

- newcomers;
- school-age mothers;
- travellers;
- looked-after children;
- children of service personnel; and
- English as an additional language.

Additional Learning Needs (Wales)
A child / young person has additional needs if:

1. A person has additional learning needs if he or she has a learning difficulty or disability (whether the learning difficulty or disability arises from a medical condition or otherwise) which calls for additional learning provisions.

2. A child of compulsory school age or a person over that age has a learning difficulty or disability if he or she:
    - ✔ has significantly greater difficulty in learning than the majority of others of the same age; or
    - ✔ has a disability for the purposes of the Equality Act 2010, which prevents or hinders him or her from making use of facilities for education or training of a kind generally provided for others of the same age in mainstream maintained schools or mainstream institutions in the further education sector.

The extra support given to children with ALN to help them learn is called additional learning provision (ALP). This must be written into a support plan called an IDP.

3. A child under compulsory school age has a learning difficulty or disability if he or she is, or would be if no additional learning provision were made, likely to be within subsection (2) when of compulsory school age.

4. A person does not have a learning difficulty or disability solely because the language (or form of language) in which he or she is or will be taught is different from a language (or form of language) which is or has been used at home.

Ref: Additional Learning Needs Code for Wales 2021.

The additional learning needs (ALN) system is the new system for supporting children and young people aged 0–25 in Wales with ALN. The ALN system is replacing the special educational needs (SEN) system and the system for supporting young people with learning difficulties and/or disabilities (LDD).

The ALN legislative framework is created by the Additional Learning Needs and Education Tribunal (Wales) Act 2018 (the ALN Act), the Additional Learning Needs Code for Wales 2021 (the ALN Code) and regulations made under the Act.

The ALN system replaces existing support plans (including statements of SEN, individual education plans (IEPs) for learners on school action/school action plus and Learning and Skills Plans (LSPs) for post-16 learners) with an Individual Development Plan (IDP).

Additional support for learning (ASL) (Scotland)
ASL is the extra or different help provided to learners who have additional support needs. Additional support for learning can take many different forms. It can include things like:

- changes to the curriculum or the way a learner is taught;
- support from a learning assistant;
- use of technology or changes to learning materials; and
- input from specialist teachers or health professionals.

The ASL Act gives learners who need extra help at school or nursery the right to get the support they need. The law does not say how much or what type of support each learner should get. Instead, their support must be 'adequate and efficient' and based on their individual needs.

Advocacy
Getting support from another person to help you express your views and wishes, and helping you stand up for your rights.

ALNCo
Additional Learning Needs Co-ordinator (Wales)

Alternative provision
Education in a setting that is not a mainstream or special school should be based on the needs of the child and can be provided through a variety of routes, including pupil referral units (PRUs).#

Anarthria and aphasia
A total absence of ability to form speech or language.

Annual review
The annual review is a process that includes a meeting where a local council, a school or a college, and some other people look at the support a child or young person gets and if it is right for them. The annual review must happen every 12 months.

Apprenticeships
Apprenticeships are paid for by the government and the employer. Learning at work through an apprenticeship scheme means getting a wage at the same time.

ASC and ASD
Autistic spectrum condition (used currently): Autistic spectrum disorder (medical terminology used for describing autism)

Some people with ASC prefer to be referred to as 'autistic'.

It is a lifelong developmental condition that affects many areas of a child's development, including:

- communication;
  - finding it difficult to express themselves;
  - struggling to understand facial expressions, gestures, tone of voice;
  - taking what people say literally;
  - difficulty understanding jokes or sarcasm;
- social interactions;
  - struggling to relate to others and knowing what to say and do in social situations;
  - difficulty making and maintaining relationships;
  - avoiding eye contact;
- imagination;

Glossary

- struggling to imagine what other people around them are thinking or feeling; and
- difficulty with imaginative play or storytelling.

A person with ASC might struggle with sensory sensitivities, changes to routines and transitioning. They may also spend a lot of time and energy focusing on a special interest in which they may become very knowledgeable.

'Asperger syndrome' (often shortened to Asperger's) is no longer used as a diagnostic term for autism and is considered controversial due to the history of Hans Asperger, which is summarised below.

Historically, Asperger syndrome was used as a diagnostic term for some autistic people who did not also have a diagnosis of a learning disability. Broadly, it is now agreed that what was referred to as Asperger syndrome is part of the autism spectrum, and there is no need for a separate term.

https://embrace-autism.com/an-introduction-to-audhd/

Assessment
An assessment is a way of determining what kind of support someone needs.

Assistive technology (AT) and augmentative and alternative communication (AAC)
Assistive technology (AT) is any item, piece of equipment, software programme or product system that is used to increase, maintain or improve functional capabilities.

Augmentative and alternative communication (AAC) refers to using communicative systems that augment a message and may be alternative to speech.

B

Brain injury
An *acquired brain injury (ABI)* covers all situations in which brain injury has occurred since birth and includes traumatic brain injury, as well as tumour, stroke, brain haemorrhage and encephalitis.

Traumatic brain injury (TBI) is an injury to the brain caused by trauma to the head (head injury). There are many possible causes, including road traffic accidents, assaults, falls and accidents.

The effects of a traumatic brain injury can be wide-ranging and depend on a number of factors such as the type, location and severity of the injury.

C

CAMHS

Child and adolescent mental health service

CAMHS is the NHS mental health service for children and young people.

CAMHS support covers depression, problems with food and eating, self-harm, abuse, violence or anger, bipolar disorder, schizophrenia, anxiety and other difficulties.

Careers education, information, advice and guidance (CEIAG)

The key areas of career development work are referred to as careers education, information, advice and guidance (CEIAG):

- Careers education: Usually in educational settings, this refers to a range of actions to educate people on the potential careers available, develop career management skills and explore their own career potential.
- Career information: Providing information, such as different job roles or the local labour market, to help clients make informed decisions.
- Career advice: Offering advice on the different pathways based on the client's needs, goals and situation.
- Career guidance: Career coaching helps the client explore their own strengths and development needs, their aspirations, barriers and needs, so the client has the self-understanding to confidently define their next steps.

Career development professional (CDP)

Assist individuals or organisations before or during career transitions to develop long- and short-term career strategies.

Also known as:

- careers adviser;
- careers coach;
- careers consultant;
- careers co-ordinator;
- career development practitioner;

- careers guidance counsellor;
- careers leader;
- IAG adviser;
- personal adviser; and
- senior employability adviser.

Carer

A family member or paid helper who regularly looks after a child, or a sick, elderly or disabled person.

Cerebral palsy (CP)

- Spastic cerebral palsy is the most common type; it is characterised by stiff and jerky movements. It can affect one or both sides of the body and ranges from mild to severe. Damage to the brain's motor cortex causes spastic CP. This area of the brain controls voluntary movement. It is also referred to as hypertonic cerebral palsy.
- Ataxic cerebral palsy causes issues with balance, co-ordination and voluntary movement (ataxia). It can result in poor muscle tone, shaky movements and difficulty with fine motor skills. Damage to the cerebellum causes ataxic cerebral palsy. This part of the brain is responsible for co-ordinating physical movement.
- Athetoid (dyskinetic) cerebral palsy (also known as non-spastic or dyskinetic cerebral palsy) includes choreoathetoid and dystonic cerebral palsies. These types of cerebral palsy cause issues with involuntary movement in the face, torso and limbs. It is characterised by a combination of hypotonia (loosened muscles) and hypertonia (stiffened muscles), which cause muscle tone to fluctuate. This type of cerebral palsy is caused by damage to the brain's basal ganglia and/or cerebellum. The basal ganglia regulate voluntary motor function and eye movement, and the cerebellum controls balance and co-ordination.
- Hypotonic cerebral palsy (also known as atonic cerebral palsy) is classified by low muscle tone that causes loss of strength and firmness, resulting in floppy muscles. Instability and floppiness in muscles can affect standing or walking.
- Mixed-type cerebral palsy. In some cases, damage to the developing brain is not confined to one location. When that happens, a child can develop more than one of the types of cerebral palsy, which is called mixed-type cerebral palsy.

Child protection
The UK's four nations – England, Northern Ireland, Scotland and Wales – each have their own framework of child protection legislation, guidance and practice to:

- identify children who are at risk of harm;
- take action to protect those children; and
- prevent further abuse from occurring.

Although the child protection systems are different in each nation, they are all based on similar principles.

Each UK nation is responsible for its own policies and laws for education, health and social welfare.

Children's human rights and UNCRC
Human rights are the basic rights and freedoms which we all have in order to live with dignity, equality and fairness, and to develop and reach our potential. Human rights are a list of things that all people – including children and young people – need in order to live a safe, healthy and happy life.

Child's plan (Scotland)
A personalised child's plan is developed when those working with the child or young person and family identify that a child or young person needs a range of extra support planned, delivered and co-ordinated. The child's plan should reflect the child or young person's voice and explain what should be improved for the child or young person, the actions to be taken and why the plan has been created.

Code of practice
England: The Special Educational Needs Code of Practice is published by the Department for Education and Skills. The code provides guidance on policies and procedures intended to enable pupils with SEN in England to reach their full potential, to be included in school communities and to make the transition to adult life successfully.

Northern Ireland: The SEN Code of Practice is statutory guidance based on the Education Order (Northern Ireland) 1996 and the Education (SEN) Regulations 2005.

Scotland: Additional support for learning: Statutory guidance is referred to as 'the code'.

Wales: The additional learning needs code explains what organisations are required to do by law to meet the additional learning needs of children and young people. This includes schools, further education institutions, local authorities and NHS bodies.

Cognition and learning
The mental process of knowing includes aspects such as awareness, perception, reasoning and judgement.

Cognitive ability (or thinking and reasoning abilities)
A term often used by psychologists instead of 'intelligence'.

Commissioning
The process by which services are planned, investment decisions are made, delivery is ensured and effectiveness is reviewed.

In England, clinical commissioning groups (CCGs) replaced primary care trusts on 1 April 2013. They were dissolved in July 2022, and their duties were taken on by the new integrated care systems (ICSs).

In Scotland, the National Services Directorate commissions specialist health services and national networks.

The Welsh Health Specialised Services Committee is evolving into the NHS Wales Joint Commissioning Committee starting 1 April 2024.

Local commissioning groups (LCGs) are responsible for the commissioning of health and social care in Northern Ireland, addressing the care needs of their local population.

Comprehension
Understanding of spoken or written material or practical situations.

Co-ordinated support plan (Scotland)
A CSP is a plan used for some pupils who need significant additional support with their learning. It is used to help professionals from different agencies work together. A CSP should set out broad and long-term goals for a pupil's education. It should be reviewed at least every 12 months.

CSPs are legal documents. This means that local authorities must prepare a CSP for pupils in their area who meet the criteria. They must also provide the support that is written in a CSP.

D

Decision support tool (DST)
The form that is used by the health worker who conducts the assessment to determine if a person is eligible for NHS Continuing Healthcare.

Developmental delay
A slower rate of development where a child learns more slowly than most children of the same age.

Differentiated curriculum
Differentiated curriculum refers to an individualised approach to teaching that caters to the diverse needs of students in a single class.

Direct payments
A payment made directly to a parent or young person to purchase specific services.

Under the Children and Families Act 2014, a direct payment may be made as part of a personal budget so that the parent or young person can buy certain services that are specified in their EHC plan. Direct payments can only be used for provision provided on the school or college premises if the school or college agrees.

Disabled
You're 'disabled' under the Equality Act 2010 if you have a physical or mental impairment that has a 'substantial' and 'long-term' negative effect on your ability to do normal daily activities.

The Equality Act doesn't apply to Northern Ireland, which uses two pieces of legislation: the Disability Discrimination Act 1995 and the Special Educational Needs and Disability (NI) Order 2005.

Down's syndrome
Down's syndrome occurs when you're born with an extra chromosome. You usually get an extra chromosome by chance, because of a change in the sperm or egg before you're born.

People who have Down's syndrome usually have some level of learning disability.

Dysarthria
A condition where you have difficulty speaking because the muscles you use for speech are weak. It can be caused by conditions that damage your brain or nerves, as well as some medicines.

Dyscalculia
A specific and persistent difficulty in understanding numbers.

Dyslexia
A learning difficulty that primarily affects the skills involved in accurate and fluent word reading and spelling. Characteristic features of dyslexia are difficulties in phonological awareness, verbal memory and verbal processing speed.

Dysphasia, also known as aphasia
Difficulty understanding words or putting them together in a sentence.

Dyspraxia – also known as developmental co-ordination disorder (DSD)
A developmental disorder affecting fine and/or gross motor coordination. It may also affect speech.

E

Education, Health and Care Plan (EHCP) (England)
An EHC plan describes the special educational needs that a child or young person has and the help that they will be given to meet them. It also includes the health and care provision that is needed. It is a legal document written by the local authority and is used for children and young people who have complex support needs.

Education and Skills Funding Agency (ESFA)
The ESFA is the government agency that funds education in England for learners between the ages of three and 19, and those with learning difficulties and disabilities between the ages of three and 25. The ESFA allocates funds to local authorities, which then provide the funding for maintained schools. The ESFA directly funds academies and free schools.

Educational psychologist (EP)
An educational psychologist looks at how a child or young person can be better supported to learn.

Epilepsy
A health condition that causes seizures.

Seizures are sudden surges of abnormal and excessive electrical activity in your brain and can affect how you appear or act.

Many different symptoms can occur during a seizure.

- Motor symptoms may include rhythmic jerking movements (clonic), muscles becoming weak or limp (atonic), muscles becoming tense or rigid (tonic), muscle twitching (myoclonus) or epileptic spasms (body flexes and extends repeatedly). There may also be repeated automatic movements, like clapping or rubbing of hands, lip-smacking or chewing, or running.
- Non-motor symptoms are usually called absence seizures (staring spells). Absence seizures can also have brief twitches (myoclonus) that can affect a specific part of the body or just the eyelids. Examples of symptoms that don't affect movement could be changes in sensation, emotions, thinking or cognition, autonomic functions (such as gastrointestinal sensations, waves of heat or cold, goosebumps, heart racing, etc.) or lack of movement (called behaviour arrest).

Equality Act 2010
Replaced previous anti-discrimination laws with a single Act. It sets out the different ways in which it's unlawful to treat someone.

F

Foetal alcohol syndrome disorder (FASD)
A condition caused by the mother consuming alcohol, resulting in abnormal brain development before birth.

Fragile X Syndrome
A genetic condition that usually affects males more severely than females. It is characterised by a range of developmental issues, including cognitive impairment.

G

Getting it right for every child (Scotland)
This is Scotland's national approach to promoting, supporting and safeguarding the wellbeing of all children and young people. It provides a consistent framework, shared language and common understanding of wellbeing. GIRFEC puts the child or young person at the heart and helps children and young people get the right support from the right people at the right time.

H

Hearing impairment (HI)
The term 'hearing-impaired' is often used to describe people with any degree of hearing loss.

Because there is a negative meaning attached to the term 'impaired', people may prefer 'Deaf', 'deaf' and 'hard of hearing'.

Higher-level teaching assistant (HLTA)
An experienced teaching assistant who plans and delivers learning activities under the direction of a teacher, and assesses, records and reports on pupils' progress.

I

Individual Development Plan (Wales)
All children and young people with an identified need that requires additional learning provision will have a mandatory Individual Development Plan (IDP). Children, young people, parents and carers will contribute to the creation and maintenance of IDPs through person-centred meetings/reviews.

The majority of IDPs for school-age children and young people will be maintained by a school. In some cases, the local authority will make decisions regarding preparing and maintaining IDPs if:

- the child/young person has a rare condition that requires specialist support that the school cannot reasonably provide;
- the school requires regular advice and support from external agencies over and above what can be reasonably arranged and;
- the child/young person requires equipment that can only be used by one pupil, cannot be reused or is beyond the reasonable resources of the school;
- the child/young person requires very intensive daily support which cannot be reasonably secured by the school through the school's delegated budget;
- the child is looked after; and
- dual-registered children/young people.

An IDP maintained by a school and one maintained by a local authority will have exactly the same statutory standing.

All IDPs will contain certain key elements and have the same basic structure, including a one-page profile, summary of needs, agreed outcomes and support.

Information, advice and guidance (IAG)
An umbrella term for support that helps people make informed choices about education and career options.

J

Job coaches and training in systematic instruction (TSI)

A job coach finds out what the work involves and then plans ways to help a young person fulfil these tasks. Support is ongoing until the employee has learnt the job. The system used by job coaches is called TSI. TSI is a holistic training method that focuses on errorless learning and painless correction. It can be used to train anyone in anything, regardless of whether they have additional needs or not, but the usual sector it has been used widely for many years is employment. TSI and the structured training method are widely recognised as one of the pivotal training methods for supporting people with additional needs in the workplace.

Job coaches provide in-work support within supported internships. They are not the same as work coaches! [Work coaches are JobCentre staff who meet with you when you claim Universal Credit to improve your chances of finding work.]

L

Lead professional

When children, young people and families require the help and support of a child's plan (Scotland), a lead professional will be needed. The lead professional is an agreed, identified person within the network of practitioners who is working alongside the child or young person and family. In most cases, the professional who has the greatest responsibility in co-ordinating and reviewing the child's plan will undertake this role.

Lacking capacity

Lacking capacity is when a person is not able to make a decision for themselves. Just because someone finds it hard to make one decision, it does not mean they are not able to make other decisions. See Chapter 11 for more about mental capacity.

Learning difficulties/disabilities

A learning disability affects how someone understands and remembers information. It is different from person to person. Some people may need more time to understand information.

Local offer (England)

A local offer is published by every local authority and provides information about the support and services that children and young people who have special educational needs and disabilities, and their families, can get. It includes information about education, health and care provision. It also gives information about training, employment and independent living.

Looked-after child (LAC): Any child who is in the care of the local authority or who is provided with accommodation by the local authority social services department for more than 24 hours.

M

Mainstream school
A school that provides education for all children, whether or not they have special educational needs or disabilities.

Mediation
A meeting to help people who disagree about something, like the support someone gets. They meet to try and find a way of agreeing about it.

There is usually someone else there to help them do this. This person is called a mediator.

Mental capacity assessment (MCA)
A mental capacity assessment is carried out to see if someone is able to make decisions. If someone cannot make a decision by themselves, they should still be supported to have their views heard.

Multi-sensory impairment (MSI)
A combination of visual and hearing difficulties (sometimes referred to as deafblindness).

N

Named person (Scotland)
This is a clear point of contact for times when children, young people and families require information, advice or help. The named person is mainly provided by health and education services and is usually someone who is known to the child, young person and family and who is well placed to develop a supportive relationship with them. Where there is a child's plan in place, the named person will work alongside the lead professional, continuing to provide general advice or support, while the lead professional will be the point of contact in relation to the plan. In some cases, the named person will also be the lead professional.

Neurodiversity
Neurodiversity is the concept that brain differences are natural variations – not deficits, disorders or impairments.

Some people's brains simply work in a different way. These differences mean they are not seen as 'neurotypical' and may be diagnosed with neurological conditions such as autism spectrum condition (ASC), dyslexia or attention deficit hyperactivity disorder (ADHD).

In the 1990s, a term was coined to describe these differences by sociologist Judy Singer: neurodiversity.

What does neurodivergent mean?

Neurodivergent was coined by the neurodiversity movement as the opposite of neurotypical.

The terms 'neurodivergent' and 'neurodivergence' are now used to describe all people whose neurological conditions mean that they do not consider themselves to be neurotypical.

Who is neurotypical?

Neurotypicality is used to describe people whose brain functions, ways of processing information and behaviours are seen to be standard.

The label is used by neurodivergent people and the neurodiversity community to refer to anyone who does not have a neurological condition – particularly conditions such as autism, ADHD and dyslexia.

NHS continuing healthcare (CHC)
A package of care that is arranged and funded solely by the NHS for individuals aged 18 and over who are not in hospital but have complex ongoing healthcare needs.

P

Parent carer forum
A parent carer forum is a representative local group of parents and carers of disabled children who work with local authorities, education, health and other providers to make sure the services they plan and deliver meet the needs of disabled children and families.

Pen profile
A pen profile is used to gain information in advance from schools regarding a student's needs.

Personal assistant (PA)
Personal assistants are approved support staff who offer a range of individual support and care.

Personal budgets and EHCPs (England)

A personal budget is a notional amount of money that would be needed to cover the cost of making the special educational provision specified in an EHC plan. You cannot have a personal budget unless you have an EHC plan. Information about the availability of personal budgets must be contained in the local authority's local offer.

Personal education plan (PEP):

An element of a care plan maintained by a local authority in respect of a looked-after child, which sets out the education needs of the child.

Personal health budget

A personal health budget is a set amount of money to spend on the support and services that will meet your health and wellbeing needs, as agreed between you (or your representative) and your local NHS team.

Person-centred reviews

Use person-centred thinking approaches to explore what is happening from the person and other people's perspectives. The review looks at what's working and not working, what's important to the person now and in the future, and agrees on outcomes for change.

Physical disability (PD)

Impairments that limit mobility.

Preparing for adulthood (PfA)

The transition of a young person leaving childhood and preparing to become an adult.

Pupil referral unit (PRU)

This is a school established and maintained by a local authority that is specially organised to provide education for children who are excluded, sick or otherwise unable to attend mainstream school.

R

Reasonable adjustments

Changes to schools, employers and other settings are required, which could include changes to physical features – for example, creating a ramp or providing extra support equipment.

Respite care

Respite care involves short-term or temporary care for a few hours or weeks, designed to provide relief to the regular caregiver.

S

Selective mutism
Selective mutism is a fear (phobia) of talking in selective situations or to certain people.

SEN support (England)
A category for young people (0–25) who need extra specialist support but not an EHC plan. This may take the form of additional support from within the school or require the involvement of specialist staff or support services. The purpose of SEN support is to help children achieve the outcomes or learning objectives that have been set for them by the school. Schools should involve parents in this process.

Special educational needs and disabilities (SEND) (England)
A child or young person who has special educational needs may:

- find it harder to learn than other people their age;
- face challenges that make it hard to attend school or college; and
- need extra or different support to learn.

Special education needs and disability information, advice and support service (SENDIASS) (England)
SENDIASS offers free information, advice and support to parents and carers of children and young people with special educational needs, and to the young people themselves. They are statutory services, which means there has to be one in every local authority.

Special educational needs co-ordinator (SENCO)
In England, the SENCO is the person at a school who is in charge of making sure students who have special educational needs or disabilities get the support they need.

Specific learning disabilities (SpLD)
An umbrella term used to cover a range of frequently co-occurring difficulties, usually dyslexia, dyspraxia, dyscalculia, ADD and ADHD.

Speech, language and communication needs (SLCN)
A wide range of difficulties related to all aspects of communication in children and young people can include difficulties with speech, understanding what others say and using language socially.

Student Awards Agency Scotland (SAAS)
Scotland's student funding agency.

Student Finance Wales
Wales' student finance agency

Supported internships (England)
Structured, work-based study programme for 16- to 24-year-olds with SEND, who have an education, health and care (EHC) plan. The core aim of a supported internship study programme is a substantial work placement, facilitated by the support of an expert job coach.

T

Tourette syndrome (TS)
Tourette syndrome is a neurological condition characterised by repeated involuntary movements and uncontrollable vocal (phonic) sounds called tics. Sometimes tics can include inappropriate words and phrases.

Symptoms generally appear before the individual is 18 years old. In addition to vocal tics, people with TS may touch other people, repeat actions obsessively or self-harm.

Tics increase and decrease in severity and periodically change in number, frequency, type and location. Symptoms may subside for weeks or months at a time and later recur.

Tics can increase with stress or anxiety but can often decrease when the person is engaged in an activity such as drumming, singing or playing sports.

Transition
A transition is **a change from one stage to another.** Most children and young people will experience transitions as they move through and between education, health or care settings and beyond into adult life.

Transition plan
A plan is drawn up at the annual review meeting, which sets out the steps needed to move from one school to another or from school/college to adult life.

Tribunal
A panel is set up to arbitrate when disagreements occur about the provision for a pupil's learning support needs or when a parent alleges discrimination on the grounds of a child's disability.

Tribunals have different names depending on where you live.

W

Wellbeing
Wellbeing is a measure of how a person is doing at a point in time and if there is any need for support. The eight wellbeing indicators in Scotland (SHANARRI) provide a framework for assessment and planning in relation to wellbeing.

Wellbeing indicators (SHANARRI – Scotland)
Safe, Healthy, Active, Nurtured, Achieving, Respected, Responsible, Included, sometimes referred to as SHANARRI. The wellbeing indicators (SHANARRI) are informed by the UNCRC.

Work coaches
Job Centre staff who meet with you when you claim Universal Credit to improve your chances of finding work.

Resources and further information

Apologies to all those we haven't given a mention to . . . there are so many fabulous resources out there! These are just some examples to illustrate what you can find if you investigate!

They are offered as a starting point for your professional curiosity, not a comprehensive list.

Impairments and conditions

Directories of conditions:

- NHS https://www.nhs.uk/conditions
- Contact A–Z https://contact.org.uk/conditions

Some useful links to find out more about . . .

ADHD https://adhduk.co.uk/about-adhd

Anarthria https://www.verywellhealth.com/what-is-anarthria-3146173 and aphasia https://www.nhs.uk/conditions/aphasia

Audhd https://embrace-autism.com/an-introduction-to-audhd

Autism:

The Autism Services Directory https://www.autism.org.uk/autism-services-directory has a useful UK-wide directory of employment services to support employees with autism:

- The National Autistic Societyhttps://www.autism.org.uk;
- Social stories https://carolgraysocialstories.com/social-stories/what-is-it;
- autism medical information https://www.nhs.uk/conditions/autism;
- autism and gender dysphoria https://www.autism.org.uk/advice-and-guidance/what-is-autism/autism-and-gender-identity
- Non-verbal Autism: *Listen* is a short film in which nonspeaking autistic people talk about how nonspeakers are represented in books, theatre and film. They provide guidance for changing the narrative. Learn more and access transcripts, translations and a toolkit here: https://communicationfirst.org/LISTEN

Brain Injury, functions and differences:

- The Brain Charity https://www.thebraincharity.org.uk/how-we-can-help/practical-help/employment-support;
- Headway https://www.headway.org.uk;
- https://www.ninds.nih.gov/health-information/public-education/brain-basics/brain-basics-know-your-brain;
- https://www.verywellhealth.com/brain-anatomy-4780506

Cerebral palsy http://www.cerebralpalsy.org.uk

Dysarthria https://www.nhs.uk/conditions/dysarthria

Dyscalculia https://www.bdadyslexia.org.uk/dyscalculia

Dyslexia

- The British Dyslexia Association https://www.bdadyslexia.org.uk including looking for work https://www.bdadyslexia.org.uk/advice/adults/looking-for-work ;
- The Dyslexia Association https://www.dyslexia.uk.net;
- Dyslexia Action https://dyslexiaaction.org.uk;
- The Dyslexia Foundation https://www.dyslexia-help.org offers a free online dyslexia screening https://www.dyslexia-help.org/dyslexia-test.

Dyspraxia https://www.nhs.uk/conditions/developmental-coordination-disorder-dyspraxia-in-adults

Hearing Impairment

- RNID https://rnid.org.uk;
- the National Deaf Children's Society https://www.ndcs.org.uk;
- Signature https://www.signature.org.uk;
- https://bda.org.uk British Deaf Association (BDA);
- Hearinglink https://www.hearinglink.org also provide a series of subtitled videos covering topics such as how the ear works, audiology appointments, tinnitus, balance issues and technology.
- SENSE https://www.sense.org.uk for everyone who is deafblind and/or living with complex disabilities.

Deaf with a capital D https://www.bbc.co.uk/ouch/opinion/d_or_d_whos_deaf_and_whos_deaf.shtml#:~:text=Deaf%20%2D%20with%20a%20capital%20%22D,part%20of%20the%20Deaf%20community

Cochlear implants or hearing aids https://www.verywellhealth.com/financial-aid-for-hearing-aids-and-cochlear-implants-1046604

Hearing loss and the voice https://www.intechopen.com/chapters/49108

Finger spelling https://royaldeaf.org.uk/wp-content/uploads/2024/05/RAD-BSL-Postcard-2024.pdf

https://royaldeaf.org.uk/earzz Smartphone alerting system

Common ear conditions: https://rnid.org.uk/information-and-support/ear-health/common-ear-conditions

Learning difficulty/disability:

- Mencap https://www.mencap.org.uk;
- Scopehttps://www.scope.org.uk ;
- bild helps those supporting people with complex needs; https://www.bild.org.uk/

Mental Health:

- Time to Change https://www.time-to-change.org.uk;
- Mind https://www.mind.org.uk;
- NHS Every Mind Matters https://www.nhs.uk/every-mind-matters/mental-wellbeing-tips/your-mind-plan-quiz;
- Samaritans https://www.samaritans.org;
- The Health and Safety Executive https://www.hse.gov.uk/stress/index.htm;
- The Department for Work and Pensions (DWP) Health, Work and Wellbeing initiative webpage https://www.hse.gov.uk/stress/index.htm ;
- Mental Health First Aid (MHFA) https://mhfaengland.org/mhfa-centre/news/MHFA-England-launches-new-Mental-Health-First-Aid-course/is an educational course which teaches people how to identify, understand and help a person who may be experiencing an episode of mental ill health.
- Mindful Employer https://www.mindfulemployer.dpt.nhs.uk provides employers with information and support for staff who have a mental health condition.

Neurodiverse and neurotypical:

- https://www.thebraincharity.org.uk/neurodivergent-neurodiversity-neurotypical-explained

- https://www.verywellhealth.com/what-does-it-mean-to-be-neurotypical-260047;
- https://doitprofiler.com/

Pathological demand avoidance https://www.pdasociety.org.uk/what-is-pda-menu/what-is-demand-avoidance

Post-traumatic stress https://www.nhs.uk/mental-health/conditions/post-traumatic-stress-disorder-ptsd/overview

Selective mutism:

- Selective mutism https://www.selectivemutism.org.uk/about-selective-mutism;
- Selective mutism as a fear (phobia) https://www.nhs.uk/mental-health/conditions/phobias/overview;
- https://spotify.link/8flq29mgRDb Podcast – Understanding Selective Mutism;
- NHS https://www.nhs.uk/mental-health/conditions/selective-mutism;
- Selective Mutism Information & Research Association (SMIRA) www.selectivemutism.org.uk;

Sensory Processing Disorder:

- https://www.griffinot.com/sensory-processing-disorder
- https://sensoryladders.org
- Sensory regulation https://autismspectrumnews.org/the-power-of-sensory-integration-enhancing-communication-for-non-speaking-individuals/#:~:text=Sensory%20regulation%20influences%20attention%20and%20focus%2C%20essential%20to,cannot%20attend%20to%20and%20focus%20on%20communication%20activities.;
- https://www.autism.org.uk/advice-and-guidance/professional-practice/sensory-differences

Vision impairment

- RNIB https://www.rnib.org.uk/living-with-sight-loss/education-and-learning/making-the-transition-from-school/transition-guide-bridging-the-gap
- Colour blindness/ Colour Vision Defects (CVD): Types of Colour Blindness https://www.colourblindawareness.org/colour-blindness/types-of-colour-blindness;

- Access strategies available for those with visual impairment https://www.visioncenter.org/resources/visual-impairment-accessibility
- Blind Person's Allowance https://www.gov.uk/blind-persons-allowance;
- SENSE https://www.sense.org.uk for everyone who is deafblind and/or living with complex disabilities.

Optical illusions:

- Monkey Business https://www.youtube.com/watch?v=IGQmdoK_ZfY
- The dress https://www.nyu.edu/about/news-publications/news/2017/april/why-did-we-see-_the-dress-differently--the-answer-lies-in-the-sh.html#:~:text=%E2%80%9CHowever%2C%20artificial%20light%20tends%20to%20be%20yellowish%2C%20so,taken%20into%20account%2C%20which%20the%20brain%20does%20continuously.%E2%80%9D
- https://www.livescience.com/health/mind/32-optical-illusions-and-why-they-trick-your-brain

Auditory illusions:

Yanni Laurel https://www.youtube.com/watch?v=1mes0WCHG3chttps://www.youtube.com/watch?v=yDiXQl7grPQ

- How to hear Laurel https://www.youtube.com/watch?v=Tz3Og4ANFDQ
- https://www.youtube.com/watch?v=yDiXQl7grPQ – explainer

The McGurk Effect :

- https://www.youtube.com/watch?v=2k8fHR9jKVM
- https://www.simplypsychology.org/mcgurk-effect.html

Co-occurance, Comorbidity and multimorbidity https://www.nice.org.uk/guidance/NG56

Assisted communication and technology

To check if a communication professional is registered, use the National Registers of Communication Professionals working with Deaf and Deafblind People (NRCPD) https://www.nrcpd.org.uk.

Sign language interpreters and deafblind interpreters in Scotland register with the Scottish Association of Sign Language Interpreters (SASLI) https://thescottishregister.co.uk or NRCPD https://www.nrcpd.org.uk, or both.

There are some good explainers on Jamie Knight's website https://spacedoutandsmiling.com

Assistive technology

You can see some examples of AAC here:

- PECS https://pecs-unitedkingdom.com/pecs;
- Liberator https://www.liberator.co.uk;
- AssistiveWare https://www.assistiveware.com/learn-aac%C2%A0 ;
- AceCentre https://acecentre.org.uk .

The National Association for Special Educational Needs (nasen) miniguide on Assistive Technology https://nasen.org.uk/resources

To organise, co-ordinate, complete and share tasks: *Asana, Remember the Milk, Due, Evernote, Dropbox, Priority Matrix, RescueTime, Wunderlist, ColorNote.*

- Budgeting: YNAB;
- Always late? Navigation apps such as *Waze;*
- Help with passwords: *LastPass;*
- Calming down: *Headspace, Calm, Breathe2Relax, BOLD Tranquility, Yoga Nidra, Naturespace.*

And some that are more costly, but specifically made for disabled people or education support needs such as:

- Brain in Hand https://braininhand.co.uk;
- https://shop.microlinkpc.com/product-category/software

If you are looking at a screen together you can change your settings to offer an accessible experience:

Apple – https://support.apple.com/accessibility

Chromebooks – https://www.google.com/chromebook/accessibility

Microsoft – https://www.microsoft.com/en-us/accessibility

Avoiding information overload

Liane Hambly – teaching skills instead of providing info https://www.youtube.com/watch?v=bzjmCmpZi0g&feature=youtu.be

Autism Virtual Reality Experience https://www.youtube.com/watch?v=DgDR_gYk_a8

https://www.autism.org.uk/advice-and-guidance/topics/mental-health/autistic-fatigue/autistic-adults

Careers offers

England https://nationalcareers.service.gov.uk/explore-careers

Northern Ireland https://www.nidirect.gov.uk/articles/how-careers-service-can-help-you

Scotland https://www.skillsdevelopmentscotland.co.uk/what-we-do/scotlands-careers-services My World of Work

Careers Wales https://careerswales.gov.wales

Communication

www.templegrandin.com

https://www.mencap.org.uk/learning-disability-explained/communicating-people-learning-disability

https://www.gov.uk/government/publications/inclusive-communication/using-a-range-of-communication-channels-to-reach-disabled-people

https://www.learningdisabilities.org.uk/learning-disabilities/a-to-z/c/communicating-people-learning-disabilities

CHANGEPeople video – How can I communicate better with people with learning disabilities https://www.youtube.com/watch?v=wuLAQOHFn2U

Ethics

https://www.agcas.org.uk/agcas-member-code-of-ethics

https://www.thecdi.net/about-us/cdi-code-of-ethics

https://www.agcas.org.uk/AGCAS-position-and-impartiality-and-the-promotion-of-particular-employers-and-industry-sectors

Inclusive by Design

What Is Inclusive Design? A Beginner's Guide [2024] (careerfoundry.com) https://careerfoundry.com/en/blog/ux-design/beginners-guide-inclusive-design;

Neurodiversity Tips: Using Whiteboards, Earbuds, Authentic Self, Pomodoro technique, Talk to your client | CXK's Careers Practitioner Tips (youtube.com) https://www.youtube.com/watch?v=3dfhn1Ep79g;

Inclusive by Design Career Posters – CXK https://www.cxk.org/resources/career-posters

Qualifications ladder: Ladder Levels (cxk.org)www.cxk.org/wp-content/uploads/2022/09/Ladder-Levels-5.pdf

Are you Open Day Ready? (cxk.org) www.cxk.org/wp-content/uploads/2023/06/Are-you-Open-Day-Ready-8.pdf

https://nda.ie/ Centre for Excellence in Universal Design,

https://business.scope.org.uk/article/subtitles-closed-captions-transcripts-and-accessibility

Text accessibility:

- https://www.bdadyslexia.org.uk/advice/employers/creating-a-dyslexia-friendly-workplace/dyslexia-friendly-style-guide
- https://disabilitease.com/best-and-worst-font-types-visually-impaired
- colorswww.cs.cmu.edu/~jbigham/pubs/pdfs/2017/colors.pdf#:~:text=McCarthy%20and%20Swierenga%20stated%20that%20poor%20color%20selections,blue%2Fyellow%20pairs%20were%20chosen%20by%20people%20with%20dyslexia.

How to Find and Enjoy Your Computer's Accessibility Settings | Microsoft Windows https://www.microsoft.com/en-us/windows/learning-center/how-to-find-computer-accessibility-settings

Get started with accessibility features on Mac – Apple Support (UK) https://support.apple.com/en-gb/guide/mac-help/mh35884/mac

Making Chromebooks accessible for people with disabilities https://www.google.com/chromebook/accessibility

Dyslexia Style Guide 2023 (PDF) https://cdn.bdadyslexia.org.uk/uploads/documents/Advice/style-guide/BDA-Style-Guide-2023.pdf?v=1680514568

Examples of info for young people:

CXK https://www.cxk.org/services/career-guidance-young-people

This is an example from Liberty: Careers (libertygroupltd.co.uk) which helps to prepare learners https://www.libertygroupltd.co.uk/careers.

Poster which explains the service in a simplified manner to help prepare students https://www.cosmic-cactus.com/general-7

Models of Disability and Disability Rights

Disability Rights UK is the UK's leading organisation led by, run by and working for disabled people. www.disabilityrightsuk.org

Right to Participate project: funded by the Legal Education Foundation. The project aims to increase awareness of the Equality Act, especially the ways it can protect disabled people from discrimination in everyday situations. https://righttoparticipate.org

Sharing and Disclosure – Disabled Students UK | Disclosure and requesting adjustments: https://disabledstudents.co.uk/resources/disclosure-and-requesting-adjustments/

Disability Rights UK | Telling people you're disabled: a clear and easy guide for students: https://www.disabilityrightsuk.org/resources/telling-people-you%E2%80%99re-disabled-clear-and-easy-guide-students

https://www.equalityhumanrights.com

https://www.disabilitywales.org/social-model

https://inclusionscotland.org/get-informed/social-model

https://www.ombudsman.org.uk/sites/default/files/FDN-218144_Introduction_to_the_Social_and_Medical_Models_of_Disability.pdf

https://www.gov.uk/government/publications/equality-act-guidance/disability-quick-start-guide-for-service-providers-html

The social model of disability – Sense https://www.sense.org.uk/about-us/the-social-model-of-disability

https://www.disabled-world.com/definitions/disability-models.php

Liberating the NHS: No decision about me, without me (publishing.service.gov.uk) https://assets.publishing.service.gov.uk/government/uploads/system/uploads/attachment_data/file/216980/Liberating-the-NHS-No-decision-about-me-without-me-Government-response.pdf

Nothing Without Us: Experiences of Disability | Pitt Rivers Museum (ox.ac.uk) https://www.prm.ox.ac.uk/event/nothing-without-us

Through the Patient's Eyes. Salzburg Seminar Session 356, 1998 https://www.salzburgglobal.org/multi-year-series/general/pageId/6381

Intersectionality:

https://www.verywellmind.com/what-is-intersectionality-7097945

https://www.disabilityrightsuk.org/resources/inclusion-and-intersectionality-online-resource-support-disabled-people%E2%80%99s-organisations

Ableism classifies entire groups of people as 'less than' https://www.youtube.com/watch?v=_b7k6pEnyQ4

https://www.theguardian.com/society/2023/jul/11/jason-arday-cambridge-university-youngest-black-professor

Support for disabled people

Disability Rights UK offers lots of useful information on access and reasonable adjustments https://www.disabilityrightsuk.org/training-consultancy.

Contact's directory of conditions will signpost you to organisations supporting specific types of impairment or disability https://contact.org.uk/conditions.

The Business Disability Forum provides fact sheets on a range of physical disabilities for their members https://businessdisabilityforum.org.uk.

Disabled Apprentice Network (DAN) brings together Disabled apprentices and those who have finished their apprenticeship. It's a lively and friendly forum to share your experiences and offer views on what could improve apprenticeships for Disabled people https://www.disabilityrightsuk.org/disabled-apprentice-network.

Circles of support:

https://www.learningdisabilities.org.uk/learning-disabilities/a-to-z/c/circles-support-and-circles-friends

http://complexneeds.org.uk/modules/Module-3.3-Promoting-positive-behaviour---maintaining-positive-relationships/All/downloads/m11p130d/LP_Practitioners_Guide.pdf

Families planning together:

https://www.togethermatters.org.uk/resources-and-information

Short lives: http://www.bdfa-uk.org.uk/wp-content/uploads/2016/08/TfSL_A_Family_Guide_to_SEND__FINAL_.pdf

Supported employment:

Information about supported employment (Easy Read www.base-uk.org/sites/default/files/info_about_supported_employment.pdf);

BASE (British Association for Supported Employment): https://www.base-uk.org/home

Advocacy:

Coram Voice have a useful Advocacy toolkit for transition https://coramvoice.org.uk/wpcontent/uploads/2020/10/Coram-Voice-Transition-Toolkit-2020-3rd-Edition-COPYv1.pdf. It has a great jargon buster section.

Providing Independent Advocacy under the Care Act – self-study pack www.local.gov.uk/sites/default/files/documents/self-study-pack-669.pdf.

A template letter parents/carers can use to ask for an assessment for their child www.local.gov.uk/sites/default/files/documents/self-study-pack-669.pdf.

Access to work:

Gov. information: www.gov.uk/government/publications/access-to-work-factsheet/access-to-work-factsheet-for-customers

Access to work: get support if you have a disability or health condition https://www.gov.uk/access-to-work.

Apply for communication support at a job interview if you have a disability or health condition (Access to Work) https://www.gov.uk/guidance/apply-for-communication-support-at-a-job-interview-if-you-have-a-disability-or-health-condition-access-to-work

In this video Diversity and Ability, Disability Rights UK and Evenbreak take you through the process of applying to Access to Work: https://www.youtube.com/watch?v=rggqzV12ziU

Maximus provide mental health support: https://atw.maximusuk.co.uk/gethelptoday

Funding:

- Funding further education for disabled students https://www.disabilityrightsuk.org/resources/funding-further-education-disabled-students;

- Funding higher education for disabled students https://www.disabilityrightsuk.org/resources/funding-higher-education-disabled-students;
- Funding postgraduate education for disabled students https://www.disabilityrightsuk.org/resources/funding-postgraduate-education-disabled-students;
- Funding from charitable trusts https://www.disabilityrightsuk.org/resources/funding-charitable-trusts.

Grants and bursaries

Grant search tools:

- Turn2us https://grants-search.turn2us.org.uk;
- Disability Grants https://www.disability-grants.org;
- Lightning Reach https://www.lightningreach.org/application-portal.

Info on general student grants, bursaries and scholarships across the UK https://www.savethestudent.org/student-finance/student-grants-bursaries-scholarships.html#fundingtypes

16–19 College Bursaries in England https://www.gov.uk/1619-bursary-fund

Disabled Students Allowance:

England https://www.gov.uk/disabled-students-allowance-dsa

disability evidence form https://assets.publishing.service.gov.uk/media/65cdfeb61d93950012946713/sfe_disability_evidence_form_o.pdf

https://www.ucas.com/undergraduate/applying-university/individual-needs/disabled-students/support-disabled-students-frequently-asked-questions

Scotland https://www.saas.gov.uk/forms/dsa

Wales https://www.studentfinancewales.co.uk/news/what-support-is-available-for-students-with-a-learning-difficulty-mental-health-condition-or-disability

Northern Ireland https://www.studentfinanceni.co.uk/types-of-finance/postgraduate/tuition-fee-and-extra-help-student/extra-help/disabled-students-allowance/what-is-it

Video: https://www.diversityandability.com/dsa-find-your-way

Support to find work:

Support to work (Scope) – a free online and telephone support programme for disabled people who are looking for paid work https://www.scope.org.uk/employment-services/support-to-work.

Sense – employment support for people with complex disabilities https://www.sense.org.uk/our-services/education-and-work/employment-support-people-with-complex-disabilities

Thomas Pocklington Trust (TPT) Employment Service – supports blind and partially sighted people wanting to start, restart or progress their careers https://www.pocklington-trust.org.uk/employment.

Evenbreak – where disabled candidates can search for jobs with inclusive employers https://www.evenbreak.co.uk/en.

Ambitious about Autism – offers autistic people aged 18 years and older the chance to showcase their skills and attributes in the workplace https://www.ambitiousaboutautism.org.uk/what-we-do/employment/paid-work-experience.

Diversity Jobs – collaborate with companies that prioritise Diversity and Inclusion, connecting candidates with the right skill set to the right employers, regardless of their background https://diversityjobsgroup.com.

Self-employment/Entrepreneurship:

Support and Mentoring Enabling Entrepreneurship https://sameecharity.org/about

https://independentandworkready.co.uk

Work and Health Programme https://www.gov.uk/work-health-programme

Work experience and volunteering:

https://www.cxk.org/resources/finding-work-experience-or-volunteering

Accessible toilets: https://nymas.co.uk/accessible-toilets-an-essential-guide

Disability Confident:

The scheme has three levels designed to support employers on their Disability Confident journey, these are:

- Disability Confident Committed (Level 1);
- Disability Confident Employer (Level 2);
- Disability Confident Leader (Level 3).

https://www.gov.uk/government/collections/disability-confident-campaign

Advice for employers on attracting, recruiting and retaining disabled people https://www.gov.uk/government/publications/employing-disabled-people-and-people-with-health-conditions

Schemes in Wales, Scotland and Northern Ireland https://www.gov.uk/education-maintenance-allowance-ema.

Reflective practice

CPD for the Career Development Professional A Handbook for Enhancing Practice Siobhan Neary and Claire Johnson https://trotman.co.uk/products/cpd-for-the-career-development-professional

www.creativecareercoaching.org/wp-content/uploads/2015/02/Technician-or-Artist.pdf

Tools to help with reflection:

https://www.thecdi.net/CDI/media/Write/Documents/CDI_How_to_Use_the_Recommendations_for_Quality_Assurance_Criteria_Career_Development_Intervention_Observation_or_Self_Reflection.pdf

https://www.cxk.org/resources/cxk-reflective-practice-tool-for-careers-practitioners [For more information see *Careers Matters*, April 2023 – Orientations for Careers Work.]

Open Partnership Model https://iet-ou.github.io/cloudworks-ac-uk/cloud/view/8815.html As published in the June 2014 edition of *Career Matters* magazine by the CDI.

Theories, books and research

https://trotman.co.uk/collections/books-for-careers-advisers

Theory – Introduction and Concepts – Marcr https://marcr.net/marcr-for-career-professionals/career-theory/career-theory-introduction-and-concepts

Introduction to Career Theory – Tristram Hooley https://www.youtube.com/watch?v=iqz1ne2l670

Career guidance for social justice – Tristram Hooley https://careerguidancesocialjustice.wordpress.com

https://creativecareercoaching.org/product/creative-career-coaching-theory-into-practice-2019/ Hambly and Bomford

https://creativecareercoaching.org/why-clients-dont-take-action-career-inaction-theoryLiane Hambly

https://creativecareercoaching.org/product/career-development-theory-handbook-for-individualsLiane Hambly

https://trotman.co.uk/products/career-development-theories-in-practice Julia Yates

A History of the Careers Services in the UK from 1999 Michelle Stewarthttps://www.lulu.com/shop/michelle-stewart/a-history-of-the-careers-services-in-the-uk-from-1999/paperback/product-p665q7j.html?q=a+history+of+careers+services&page=1&pageSize=4

http://thepromisefoundation.org/career-and-livelihood-planning

https://counsellingtutor.com/counselling-approaches/person-centred-approach-to-counselling/carl-rogers-core-conditions

https://careerswriters.com/2024/04/17/risk-and-decision-making

https://www.choosingtherapy.com/adhd-brain-vs-normal-brain

Subcortical brain volume differences in participants with attention deficit hyperactivity disorder in children and adults: https://www.thelancet.com/journals/lanpsy/article/PIIS2215-0366(17)30049-4/abstract

https://www.nih.gov/news-events/news-releases/brain-matures-few-years-late-adhd-follows-normal-pattern

'differentialism' Realistic, Investigative, Artistic, Social, Enterprising, Conventional https://www.careerkey.org/fit/personality/realistic-career.

http://thepromisefoundation.org/career-and-livelihood-planning

What is Career Development?: https://www.thecdi.net/about-us/career-development-and-the-cdi/what-is-career-development

What is Pedagogy? https://www.youtube.com/watch?v=QcpwEoW1uY8

Briefing Paper July 2021 Understanding the role of the careers adviser within 'Personal Guidance' Dr Michelle Stewart (CDI 119-Role of a Careers Adviser-2021.indd (thecdi.net)) www.thecdi.net/CDI/media/Write/Documents/CDI_119-Role_of_a_Careers_Adviser-2021-FINAL_v_to_use.pdf?ext=.pdf

When Do We Know (youtube.com) https://www.youtube.com/watch?v=QLG55zbJIvg

Transactional Analysis https://www.simplypsychology.org/transactional-analysis-eric-berne.html

Loose Parts for Children with Diverse Abilities Miriam Beloglovsky | November 2022 https://www.communityplaythings.co.uk/learning-library/articles/loose-parts-for-diverse-abilities

Social stories and comic strip conversations

- Timmins, Dr. S. (2017) *Successful Social Stories for School and College Students with Autism*, Jessica Kingsley Publishers.
- Gray, C. (2015) *The New Social Story Book: 15th Anniversary Edition*. Future Horizons Firm.
- Gray, C. (1994) *Comic Strip Conversations: Illustrated Interactions with Students with Autism and Related Disorders Carol Gray Social Story Sampler*. Future Horizons Incorporated.
- Gerhardt, P., Cohen, M. (2014) *Visual Supports for People with Autism: A Guide for Parents and Professionals*. Woodbine House.
- Howley, M., Arnold, E. (2005) *Revealing the Hidden Social Code*. Jessica Kingsley Publishers.

Growth mindset

Carol Dweck's TED talk about Growth Mindset: https://www.ted.com/talks/carol_dweck_the_power_of_believing_that_you_can_improve

https://www.psychologytoday.com/us/basics/growth-mindset

ReFraming

https://www.verywellmind.com/reframing-defined-2610419

Mindfulness

Square breathing https://www.childline.org.uk/toolbox/calm-zone/#breathing_ipnav52832

Mental Capacity

This video explains the Mental Capacity Act in the context of young people youtu.be/tsthYJV0yig

Social Care best practice – with some fabulous video explainers: https://www.scie.org.uk/mca/introduction/mental-capacity-act-2005-at-a-glance

Mental Capacity Act Gov. info https://www.gov.uk/government/publications/mental-capacity-act-code-of-practice

Mental Capacity Act 2005 MINDhttps://www.mind.org.uk/information-support/legal-rights/mental-capacity-act-2005/overview/

Independent Mental Capacity Advocates (IMCAs)?

- What is an IMCA?
- When am I entitled to an IMCA?
- How can an IMCA help me?
- https://www.mind.org.uk/information-support/guides-to-support-and-services/advocacy/imcas/

MCA Factsheet: https://councilfordisabledchildren.org.uk/sites/default/files/uploads/files/pfa_factsheet_-_mca.pdf

https://learning.nspcc.org.uk/child-protection-system/gillick-competence-fraser-guidelines

Action planning

Reflections on a conversation with Jules Benton 2021 by Liane Hambly https://creativecareercoaching.org/inclusive-action-planning-reflections-on-a-conversation-with-jules-benton-2021/

Career or route mapping https://www.youtube.com/watch?v=4wRaWU6M7Nc).

In 2021 Liz Reece wrote a highly informative position paper for the CDI on action planning which can be found here: CDI 93-Briefing Career Action Planning.indd (thecdi.net) https://www.thecdi.net/CDI/media/Write/Documents/Briefing_Paper_-_Career_Action_Planning-web.pdf?ext=.pdf

An example of the Action Plans CXK use can be found here: Career Guidance for Young People: Supporting Your Next Steps (cxk.org) https://www.cxk.org/services/career-guidance-young-people/

Person-Centred Planning

An easy-to-follow animation to explain the Person-Centred Planning meeting https://www.youtube.com/watch?v=D9n5EzYIwKA

Decision-making profile https://www.ndti.org.uk/assets/files/Planning-My-Future-Life-Helpful-Tools-Editable.pdf

The first of series of Person-Centred Planning videos on YouTube: https://www.youtube.com/watch?v=pTl7Rvdi-_g

An example of Person-Centred planning described on a Local Offer https://www.westsussex.gov.uk/tools-for-schools/childs-journey/person-centred-planning

PATH and MAPS

https://inclusive-solutions.com/person-centred-planning/path

https://inclusive-solutions.com/person-centred-planning/maps

Preparing for Adulthood

resources.careersandenterprise.co.uk/resources/gatsby-benchmark-toolkit-send

councilfordisabledchildren.org.uk/transition-information-network

nationalcareers.service.gov.uk/careers-advice/options-with-education-health-andcare-plan/

https://www.disabilityrightsuk.org/resources/resources-index

https://www.ndti.org.uk/resources/preparing-for-adulthood-all-tools-resources

gov.uk/topic/schools-colleges-childrens-services/special-educational-needsdisabilities

riseabove.org.uk emotional resilience and health information

https://www.youtube.com/user/rolemodelsinspire/videos inspire a generation disabilitymatters.org.uk/ free e-learning resource

https://resources.careersandenterprise.co.uk/resources/transition-programmesyoung-adults-send-what-works templates from NDTi: https://www.ndti.org.uk/resources/preparing-for-adulthood-all-tools-resources

- One Page Profile
- What Matters Island
- Inclusion Web
- Good Day / Bad Day
- Perfect Week
- Decision Making Profile
- Communication Passport
- Matching Support
- Presence to Contribution
- Like & Admire
- Relationship Map
- Important to / Important for
- Working / Not Working
- My Outcomes
- Summary Vocational Profile, One page (pdf for printing)
- Summary Vocational Profile, One Page (editable pdf)
- Vocational Profile, Full (pdf for printing)
- Vocational Profile, Full (editable pdf)

CXK: include their Careers Ladder and Post 16 Options posters (found on their website and available for free at: https://www.cxk.org/wp-content/uploads/2022/09/Ladder-Levels-5.pdf and https://www.cxk.org/wp-content/uploads/2022/09/GCSE-Options-Poster.pdf) and CXK Careers Hub: https://view.publitas.com/youth-employability-service/cxk-careers-home/page/1

A video for Career Mapping: https://www.youtube.com/watch?v=4wRaWU6M7Nc

Many other Careers companies offer free resources – we've just used CXK as an example because Chris works there and features in their videos ☺

Card sorts

https://sunrisecareerguidance.co.uk/shapeofcareercards

https://panjango.com/products/panjango-trumps

https://whatsyourstrength.co.uk

https://creativecareercoaching.org/product/career-navigator-bronze-membership

You can also use Career Navigator digitally! https://creativecareercoaching.org/online-card-sort-silver-career-navigator-liane

Examples of Insight videos, podcasts and Massive Open Online Courses (MOOCs)

Videos by Kent & Medway Progression Federation aimed at students with additional needs who are considering university: https://kmpf.org/resources.

These are a must listen for any careers professional supporting students with additional needs, especially those who are researching and applying to university: https://shows.acast.com/6582c6de05fe7800152c7b39

KMPF do a great job of sourcing additional links too: https://kmpf.org/schools-and-colleges/sen-progression-partnership/send-pp-disability-links

The award-winning short film *Listen* in which nonspeaking autistic people talk about how nonspeakers are represented and provide guidance for changing the narrative. Learn more and access transcripts, translations and a toolkit here: https://communicationfirst.org/LISTEN

The One in Five Podcast – shares experiences of higher education https://shows.acast.com/the-one-in-5-podcast.

Massive Open Online Courses (MOOCs) are free online courses.

https://www.futurelearn.com/info/blog/what-is-a-mooc-futurelearn

A Life in Careers – Chris interviews Malcolm Scott https://www.youtube.com/watch?v=JvHKDwDdjto

Autism TMI Virtual Reality Experience https://www.youtube.com/watch?v=DgDR_gYk_a8

Country-specific resources:

England

https://www.gov.uk/government/publications/participation-of-young-people-education-employment-and-training

What is an EHCP and an IEP, and how can my child get one? – Support for Parents from Action For Children https://parents.actionforchildren.org.uk/school-life/special-education-needs-disabilities-send/ehcp-iep

The SEND Code of Practice

Statutory 'must do's: https://www.ndti.org.uk/resources/changedevelopment-project/must-dos-send-code-of-practice

ESFA Adult Education Budget Learning Support. https://www.gov.uk/discretionary-learner-support/overview

https://www.gov.uk/government/publications/send-19-to-25-year-olds-entitlement-to-ehc-plans/send-19-to-25-year-olds-entitlement-to-ehc-plans

What can college offer young people with Special Educational Needs and Disabilities? https://natspec.org.uk/wp-content/uploads/2021/12/SE19-SEND-Network_Further-education-resource_Digital_Final.pdf

https://www.gov.uk/government/publications/send-19-to-25-year-oldsentitlement-to-ehc-plans/send-19-to-25-year-olds-entitlement-to-ehc-plans

Requesting an Education, Health and Care needs assessment https://www.ipsea.org.uk/ehc-needs-assessments

Local offer guide https://councilfordisabledchildren.org.uk/sites/default/files/uploads/files/Local%2520Offer%2520Guide.pdf

Special Needs Jungle useful flow chart https://specialneedsjungle.com/wp-content/uploads/2018/10/SNJ-FLOWCHART3x-2018.pdf

SENDIASS: Find your local Information Advice and Support service – As part of the Children and Families Act 2014 it is a legal requirement that all local authorities ensure children and young people with Special Educational Needs and Disabilities (SEND) and their parents have access to an impartial Information, Advice and Support (IAS) service. https://councilfordisabledchildren.org.uk/about-us-0/networks/information-advice-and-support-services-network/find-your-local-ias-service

You can use the IPSEA website to find out information about:

- SEN support at school or college;
- EHC needs assessments and EHC plans;
- Transport to school or college.

https://www.ipsea.org.uk/pages/category/education-health-and-care-plans

Supported Internships Easy Read guide https://www.base-uk.org/sites/default/files/knowledge/Supported%20Internships%20guidance

%20-%20easy%20read/supported_interships_guidance_for_learners_8th_april_2014.pdf

Supported Internships and self-employment https://www.ndti.org.uk/resources/publication/sis_and_self-employment

https://www.ndti.org.uk/resources/internships-work-all-resources/internships-work-resources-for-young-people-families

Apprenticeships – more flexible requirements for Maths and English https://www.base-uk.org/inclusive-apprenticeships

https://amazingapprenticeships.com/app/uploads/2018/08/Apps_A5_Learner_Support.pdf

(https://www.base-uk.org/inclusive-apprenticeships).

For SENCOs: https://www.careersandenterprise.co.uk/schools/senco-module

Specialist Colleges https://natspec.org.uk/colleges/specialist-colleges

The Care Act https://www.legislation.gov.uk/ukpga/2014/23/contents

Do you Care? https://www.ndti.org.uk/resources/publication/do-you-care-preparing-carers-to-get-the-best-from-the-care-act-2014

Supporting pupils at school with medical conditions (2014) Updated 2017: statutory guidance from the Department for Education https://www.gov.uk/government/publications/supporting-pupils-at-school-with-medical-conditions--3

Children and Families Act 2014 https://www.legislation.gov.uk/ukpga/2014/6/contents

Student Finance England https://studentfinance.campaign.gov.uk

https://www.scie.org.uk/mca/introduction/mental-capacity-act-2005-at-a-glance

Wales

In Wales, you can get an Individual Development Plan (IDP). This has replaced the Statement of Special Educational Needs https://www.snapcymru.org/get-support/idps/.

https://www.ndti.org.uk/resources/publication/person-centered-planning---wales

https://www.gov.wales/special-educational-needs

https://www.gov.wales/sites/default/files/publications/2024-04/220622-the-additional-learning-needs-code-for-wales-2021%20%282%29.pdf

https://careerswales.gov.wales/my-future/support-for-parents-and-carers/helping-your-child-plan-their-future/additional-learning

Apprenticeships: a guide for disabled learners https://www.gov.wales/apprenticeships-guide-disabled-learners

Visit Apprenticeships. A Genius Decision (external website) for more information and videos about being an apprentice. https://www.gov.wales/apprenticeships-genius-decision

Watch videos on the Engage To Change YouTube channel to find out more about the employment support available to young people in Wales. https://www.youtube.com/@engagetochange3690

Support Finder – search for programmes that can help you improve your skills and work opportunities https://careerswales.gov.wales/support-finder

My Future – easy to read careers information https://careerswales.gov.wales/my-future .

CareersCraft on Minecraft https://careerswales.gov.wales/education-and-teaching-professionals/teaching-and-learning-resources/careerscraft-on-minecraft

Transition to adult services

https://www.gov.wales/sites/default/files/publications/2022-02/transition-handover-guidance-children-adult-services-young-peoples-version.pdf

Social Services and Well-being (Wales) Act 2014 https://socialcare.wales/resources-guidance/information-and-learning-hub/sswbact/overview

SNAP Cymru works with families and professionals to ensure that young people's needs are identified and provision made available to help them reach their potential. https://www.snapcymru.org/

Scope Cymru offers free and confidential information, advice and support for disabled people, their families and professionals in Wales on a variety of issues. For disability information call 0808 800 3333. https://www.scope.org.uk

Contact a Family Cymru is a charity that works across Wales to support families of children with disabilities or additional needs, whatever their condition or disability. Free phone helpline: 0808 808 3555. https://contact.org.uk

Learning Disability Wales is a national charity representing the learning disability sector in Wales. It works with people with a learning disability, government and the voluntary sector to create a better Wales for people with a learning disability.http://www.ldw.org.uk

Children in Wales provides services for those working with children, young people and families in Wales. They aim to improve the lives of them all, but especially those affected by family instability, poverty and deprivation or have special needs/disabilities. https://www.childreninwales.org.uk

Mencap Cymru is a charity for people with learning disabilities. They also support families and carers. Their aim is to change the world for everyone with a learning disability. https://wales.mencap.org.uk

Specialist Colleges https://natspec.org.uk/colleges/specialist-colleges

The Care Act

Do you Care? https://www.ndti.org.uk/resources/publication/do-you-care-preparing-carers-to-get-the-best-from-the-care-act-2014

Children and Families Act 2014 Territorial Extent and Application:https://www.legislation.gov.uk/ukpga/2014/6/contents

https://www.studentfinancewales.co.uk

https://www.scie.org.uk/mca/introduction/mental-capacity-act-2005-at-a-glance

Guide to help understand issues surrounding young people or parents of children who lack capacity in the ALN system https://educationtribunal.gov.wales/sites/educationtribunal/files/2021-08/ETW10-young-people-or-parents-of-children-who-lack-capacity.pdf

Northern Ireland

Careers Service in Northern Ireland https://www.nidirect.gov.uk/campaigns/careers

https://www.nidirect.gov.uk/articles/career-planning-young-people-special-educational-needs https://www.nidirect.gov.uk/articles/careers-guidance-interview#:~:text=A%20careers%20guidance%20interview%20is,no%20right%20or%20wrong%20answers.

Statement of Special Educational Needs. https://www.nidirect.gov.uk/articles/special-educational-needs-statements

https://www.nidirect.gov.uk/articles/children-special-educational-needs

The DE website has information and guidance for SEN and Medical Categories. https://www.education-ni.gov.uk/publications/sen-and-medical-categories-guidance-schools

The SEN Code of Practice (1998) is statutory guidance based on the Education Order (Northern Ireland) 1996 and the Education (SEN) Regulations 2005. https://www.legislation.gov.uk/nisi/1996/274/contents

The Education Order (Northern Ireland) 1996 – provides the current definitions for SEN and SEN Provision. https://www.legislation.gov.uk/nisi/1996/274/contents

Transition to adult services

https://www.nidirect.gov.uk/articles/moving-adulthood

Children and Families Act 2014 Territorial Extent and Application: https://www.legislation.gov.uk/ukpga/2014/6/contents

Student Finance Northern Ireland https://www.studentfinanceni.co.uk

Information for disabled young people: https://www.nidirect.gov.uk/information-and-services/people-disabilities

- Everyday life and leisure;
- Learning and education;
- Moving into adulthood;
- Your Transition Plan – preparing for the future;
- Education Authority Transitions Service.

Additional educational needs refer to various groups of children and young people who for a variety of reasons may face additional barriers to education and learning. This makes it more difficult for them to achieve their full potential. This is different to children with Special Educational Needs.

These areas include:

- Anti-Bullying Programme;
- Asylum Seekers and Refugees;
- Children in the juvenile justice system;
- Children of Services Personnel;
- Education Otherwise Than At School (EOTAS);
- Newcomer pupils;
- Nurture Programme;
- Pupil suspensions and expulsions;
- Review of Restraint and Seclusion;
- Roma pupils;
- School Age Mothers' Programme;
- Traveller pupils;
- Young Carers;

https://www.carersuk.org/help-and-advice/practical-support/mental-capacity-explained-northern-ireland

Scotland

In Scotland, you can apply for a Co-ordinated Support Plan. https://enquire.org.uk/parents/getting-support/co-ordinated-support-plans

Getting it right for every child (GIRFEC). https://www.gov.scot/policies/girfec

The Education (Additional Support for Learning) (Scotland) Act 2004. https://www.legislation.gov.uk/asp/2004/4/contents

Additional support for learning: statutory guidance 2017 https://www.gov.scot/publications/supporting-childrens-learning-statutory-guidance-education-additional-support-learning-scotland provides guidance on all aspects of the 2004 Act and is a code of practice for education authorities.

- Additional support for learning: guidance on assessing capacity and considering wellbeing.
- *My Rights My Say* https://myrightsmysay.scot – a children's service supporting children aged 12–15 to use their rights. They provide advice and information, advocacy support, legal representation and a service to independently seek children's views about the support they receive with their learning.
- Reach https://reach.scot– a website dedicated to children and young people aiming to help them feel supported, included, listened to and

involved in decisions at school. It has information and advice for pupils about their rights to additional support for learning; practical tips for all sorts of school problems; young people's real-life stories; and positive examples of pupil participation.

Transition to adult services – https://www.gov.scot/publications/supporting-disabled-children-young-people-and-their-families/pages/transitions

Mental Health resource to help employers support apprentices https://www.apprenticeships.scot/for-employers/mental-health-resource

Mental Health resource designed for apprentices. https://www.apprenticeships.scot/become-an-apprentice/mental-health-resource

LEAD Scotland https://www.lead.org.uk/support-for-disabled-people-to-learn

LEAD Scotland provides free learning, befriending and helpline services across Scotland for disabled people and carers.

Disability Information Scotland https://www.disabilityscot.org.uk/work-area/education-training-employment

ARC Scotland https://arcscotland.org.uk

ARC Scotland works alongside people who need additional support, and their families. This includes people with learning disabilities, autism, mental health difficulties, sensory or physical disabilities.

Compass webpage. Compass is an online tool to help young people in Scotland, their parents and carers, and the professionals who support them, with the transition to young adult life. https://www.compasslaunch.scot

Students Awards Agency Scotland SAAS Disabled Students' Allowance Money to support you while you study either full-time or part-time college and university courses. https://www.saas.gov.uk

ILF Scotland Transition Fund https://ilf.scot/transition-fund/what-is-it

Get up to £1,500 towards learning or other activities if you're a disabled person between the age of 19 and 25.

Employment and Support Allowance (ESA) https://www.gov.uk/employment-support-allowance

Students can claim ESA. It's a weekly payment if you have a disability or health condition that affects how much you can work.

Young Persons' free bus travel card https://www.transport.gov.scot/concessionary-travel/under-22s-free-bus-travel

If you're younger than 22 or disabled, you can get free bus travel across Scotland. Use this to get to and from your college, university or other training course.

Enable https://www.enable.org.uk

Enable is a charity which strives to deliver an equal society for every citizen. They have many different roles, including:

- campaigning for disabled people's rights;
- working alongside people who face barriers to getting a job;

Student Space – life as a disabled student https://studentspace.org.uk/wellbeing/life-as-a-disabled-student

Get advice on Student Space, including stories from other students, on how you can approach the challenges of student life.

Welcome pack for care-experienced apprentices. www.skillsdevelopmentscotland.co.uk/media/50dpcbch/guide-for-care-experienced-apprentices.pdf

This pack gives useful information and some insights from apprentices who have experience of the care system.

UCAS support https://www.ucas.com/apprenticeships/support-care-experienced-people-taking-apprenticeships

UCAS gives details of what you need to know if you're interested in an apprenticeship as a care-experienced student.

SAAS Care Experienced Students' Bursary https://www.saas.gov.uk/full-time/support-for-care-experienced-students

Tuition fees and a bursary for care-experienced students on full-time undergraduate (degree) courses. The Student Awards Agency Scotland (SAAS) is Scotland's student funding agency.

Who Cares? Scotland https://www.whocaresscotland.org

Who Cares? Scotland works with young people in Scotland who have experience of being in care. They listen to you and help make sure you're safe, healthy and supported.

Children and Families Act 2014 Territorial Extent and Application: https://www.gov.scot/publications/adults-with-incapacity-act-principles

Afterword and acknowledgements

P.S.
P.S. is an abbreviation for 'postscript'.
It derives from the Latin word 'postscriptum', which roughly translates to 'write after'.

Lots of people helped us to write this book! Thanks to:

- All the clients we have worked with – for their contribution to our learning and for bringing joy to our work.
- Our colleagues, who continue to develop and share best practice. This book wouldn't have been possible without you.
- Schools, Colleges and Alternative Provision across Kent and Dorset – for inviting us to work with you. With special thanks to Liberty Training, Goldwyn Group, NWKAPs, St George's C of E Foundation School, Cranbrook School, Wye School, The Duke of York's Royal Military School and KMPF SEND PP.
- CXK – for their unconditional support for this book, but also for supporting Chris in his career and being an organisation that keeps people at the heart of practice.
- Ansbury Guidance – who supported Jules and her work for many happy years.
- Sophie – who encouraged Chris to access support for ADHD.
- Liane – who, through persistence and patience, finally got Jules to write a book.
- Emma – who inspired Chris to use what he knows to help others in their careers work.
- Olly – for being encouraging, supportive and bringing us together to collaborate on this book.
- Claire – for the super-useful suggestions.
- Our families – for understanding and being there.
- The CDI – for their contribution to our learning and support for our profession.
- Trotman – for publishing this book.
- Our brains – for being the complex things they are.
- The wonderful careers community.
- You – for reading our book!

And before we sign off, we'd like to encourage you to join us in continuing to learn about the diversity of human beings and their career planning.

We hope you can use our book to help you:

- Try things out – give things a go. It may not feel comfortable, and it might not be easy (it never is when we challenge old habits), but consider how much it may benefit the clients we serve and how much it may improve their lives.
- Having tried things out . . . consider coming back to our book in a few months' time and re-reading sections that resonated or challenged you.
- Identify your own future professional development needs.
- Tell us, and the CDI, what you would you like to know more about.
- Plan to use some of the resources.
- Reflect on your own practice and make adjustments.
- Reduce any anxiety you or your clients might experience.
- Regulate, Relate and Communicate.
- Celebrate, Advocate and Navigate.
- Evaluate, Investigate and Collaborate.
- Activate, Accommodate and Create.
- Have fun learning!!

Here are a few questions you may want to ask yourself and reflect on:

What is one thing you will do differently?

What is one thing you will experiment with outside your comfort zone?

What do you need to read up on further and/or who do you need to speak to on your Continuing Professional Development journey?

How have your reflections or perspectives changed (or not)? Why might this be?

Lifelong learning can feel like a continual circle; however, from our perspective (and that of some psychologists), it is more like a slinky or a spiral. We tread the same paths day on day, but we are not travelling in a circle . . .

Afterword and Acknowledgements

rather a rising spiral, building on what we have learnt and tried in previous cycles.

Keep on trying things. It's okay if strategies don't work the first time. We call our work 'careers practice' for a reason. It's all about practice.

We wish you well with your journey, wherever you may be. We really hope to meet some of you (our readers) in the future and compare notes on the wonderful world of careers.

#SoMuchMoreThanTalkingAboutJobs

Take care and all the best!

Jules and Chris
September 2024

Demonstrate Information Intersectional Transition Acknowledge Opportunities Important Prepare Celebrate Explain Understood Agency Navigate Future Independent Rights Risk Human Consider Inspire Career Advocate Balance Motivate Decisions Practice Perspective Joy Regulate Develop Authentic Think Support Why Yourself With Flex Engage Access Safe Matter Strength Questions Sense Imagine Impartial Model Hope Ethics Review Adjust Yet Wonder How Discover Picture Challenge Connect Learn Aspire Lego Believe Diverse Values Theory Person Able Can Include Brain Feel Reflect Possible Discuss Map Relate Investigate Respect Do Share Ideas Confidential Time Path Play Dialogue Activate Consent One Parallel What Words Listen Notice Equal Circle Space Value Choice Negotiate Design Pedagogy Re-frame Affirm Communicate See Voice Collaborate Format Plan Accommodate Stories Transparent Alternative Experience Journey Create Upskill Structure Capacity Perceive Evaluate Approach Location Individual Confidence Environment Conversations Equality

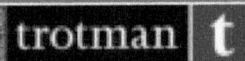

DISCOVER THE COMPLETE CAREER DEVELOPMENT SERIES

The Career Development Handbook
Tristram Hooley, Rosie Alexander and Gill Frigerio

An authoritative guide to the career development profession, outlining the key skills and knowledge used by qualified career development professionals. Includes case studies, resources and reflection points.

9781911724261 | £34.99

Career Development and Inclusive Practice
Jules Benton and Chris Targett

This engaging handbook helps career development professionals adapt their practice to support those with Special Educational Needs and Disabilities throughout their career.

9781911724285 | £34.99

Career Development Theories in Practice
Julia Yates

This indispensable guide for careers development professionals and students introduces the key career development theories accessibly, providing strategies for incorporating them into practice.

9781911724308 | £34.99

For more careers books, free resources, competitions and offers visit www.trotman.co.uk

www.ingramcontent.com/pod-product-compliance
Lightning Source LLC
Chambersburg PA
CBHW061926290426
44113CB00024B/2827